THE DINNER SALAD COOKBOOK

THE Dinner Salad

COOKBOOK

EASY & SATISFYING RECIPES THAT MAKE A MEAL

Nicole Pavlovsky

PHOTOGRAPHY BY VICTORIA WALL HARRIS

ROCKRIDGE
PRESS

To my family
and all my taste testers

CONTENTS

EUROPEAN-INSPIRED SALADS 51

AMERICAN-INSPIRED SALADS 123

INTRODUCTION

This book is an ode to salads and to living deliciously, globally, and simply.

I spent my formative years in Israel, a nation of immigrants, and I was exposed to different people of different backgrounds. I was enamored of the open-air markets and local bakeries. I can picture from memory the piles of spices, the olives marinated in various herbs, the cheeses, the serving platters of hummus, and the smell of freshly baked pita.

Later on, my family immigrated to the United States. Both my parents worked, and it was my tradition, with my mom, to make dinner for my dad and brother while watching Rachael Ray's *30 Minute Meals* on Food Network. In a world where getting anything on the dinner table is difficult after a long, stressful day at work, my family's commitment to home-cooked meals became the foundation of my food passions. Busy schedules prevent many of us from having fun in the kitchen and eating healthily; that's where the idea for quick, easy dinner salads came about. No excuses—just delicious, filling, and easy salads!

Wait, you may ask, a salad for dinner? Absolutely! Salads have a reputation for being "skinny," boring sides that are unsatisfying. Nothing could be further from the truth.

People often say that America is the melting pot of cultures and food; I think of it more as a vibrant tossed salad, full of different textures, flavors, and colors that come together to create the perfect bite. For this outlook, I thank my dad, who exposed me to different cultures and encouraged me to try new foods and travel the world. Because of this I've always felt like a global citizen, influenced and inspired by every remote corner of the world. All of the recipes in this book are inspired by a place I've lived in or traveled to, and they are satisfying dinner salads I make quickly after work.

When I lived in New Jersey and visited New York City, I was impressed by people's strong ties to their heritage. Between the Russians in Brooklyn's Brighton Beach and the large Indian population in the town where I lived, my interest in different cultures grew stronger. I spent my college years in Southern California, on the beach in Santa Barbara, and was introduced to the revolutionary concepts of avocado toast, Baja-style fish tacos, and acai bowls. The town's commitment to fitness and well-being taught me about mindful eating, self-care, and how food plays into a truly balanced life. I keep those inspirations in mind when I explore new combinations of ingredients to use in my salads.

And now, living in the Bay Area in California, I'm back in another melting pot. It's like discovering a whole new world. I've been introduced to ramen, pho, and dim sum—oh, my. My inspiration remains ignited, and I love experimenting with new ideas for quick, easy, and delicious dinner salads.

Gone are the days of iceberg lettuce, a few red onion slices, and tasteless tomatoes. It's time to say hello to vibrant salads that can be made quickly every day, with few ingredients, for a simple, delicious, and satisfying dinner. Follow along on my journey around the world as we make extraordinary salads together. No passport required.

PART I

FORMULAS FOR SALAD SUCCESS

A great dinner salad is more—so much more—than a few greens, maybe some chopped vegetables, and a heavy or oily dressing weighing down the ingredients. The key to making a great salad, one that is hearty, satisfying, and delicious, is balancing the many parts, flavors, and textures. This section is going to teach you how to make a divine salad and dressing. There's a very simple and basic formula for creating the foolproof dinner salad—one you'll use over and over again. The beauty of following it is that it makes it even easier to put together your creation on a busy weeknight, when you want a reliable stable of fantastic salads to make on the regular and you're bored of the same-old, same-old. It really is the formula for salad success.

CHAPTER 1

THE DINNER SALAD FORMULA

Why is a composed salad at a restaurant so much more crave-worthy than one we make at home? And why are the bowls at fresh fast-food joints like Chipotle and Dig Inn so much more filling than most salads? One simple reason: These places use a formula to make their salads super delicious and also hearty enough for dinner.

It's easy to see the formula at work at Chipotle, since you choose what goes into your bowl. Brown or white rice, grilled or braised meats, fresh salsas, lettuce, and cooked veggies are among the healthy options that are provided quickly and efficiently in a systematic food line. It's changed the meaning of quick, substantial meals and is the basis of the salad formula.

The salad recipes in this book follow a simple formula that ensures your salads are hearty and varied enough to be stand-alone dinners. The formula is as reliable as it is easy to follow and remember. Recipes in this book will do all the work for you when it comes to assembling the perfect dinner salad. But for those days when you don't have time to crack open this book or follow a recipe, the salad formula will make it easy for you to whip together whatever you have in your refrigerator. The formula uses four ingredients to compose a well-rounded salad, and a fifth bonus ingredient that can be modified based on your tastes, cravings, and dietary needs.

THE DINNER SALAD FORMULA

The perfect salad can be divided into a few main components, and it's simple arithmetic.

That's it. With these components, you can create a winning, simple, and satisfying salad every time. The components that make up the base, veggie/fruit, protein, and topping are the basic composition for building a salad. The bonus component is up to you, allowing you to create a salad that fits your tastes, cravings, or dietary needs.

The Salad Base

The base is the foundation of the salad bowl or plate. It is typically some type of salad green or a grain, but it can be stretched to include legumes, such as black, kidney, pinto, chickpea, or other beans. The base sets the tone for the rest of the salad, providing the body and structure.

Arugula/rocket/rucola/roquette. This green is peppery and slightly bitter, and is often used in Mediterranean cooking. It is firm and a fantastic base for richer, fattier proteins such as steak or lean seafood.

Baby spinach. A superfood, spinach is one of the most commonly eaten salad greens. It absorbs dressings and moisture well without getting soggy, and it is mild in flavor.

Butterhead lettuce/butter lettuce/Boston lettuce/Bibb lettuce. Butterhead lettuce is the overarching name for the butter, Boston, and Bibb varieties. Each is a mild head lettuce that has a smooth texture. They pair well with most flavors and are often used for lettuce wraps.

Cabbage. This can come in purple, green, or white color variations, and is great for pickling, fermenting, steaming, stewing, braising, or just adding to salads raw. Depending on its method of preparation and the color chosen, cabbage can be sour, salty, or bitter.

Frisée. This is a very leafy, bushy green that is often confused with endive. It is slightly bitter and adds a ton of texture in salads. It pairs well with bold flavors and can hold dressings well without getting soggy.

Iceberg lettuce. This lettuce gets a bad rap compared to the rest of its salad cousins as it is typically used in wedge-type salads and as the sad topping on fast food. Iceberg lettuce is known to be less nutritiously dense than other varieties, but it still contains vitamins and antioxidants. It has a higher water content than other lettuces and is very mild in flavor. I personally don't use iceberg in my salads, and it's not part of the recipes in this book. I prefer to use romaine or butter lettuce if a neutral-tasting lettuce is called for.

Kale. The hype with this green is well deserved. This superfood is loaded with phytochemicals and vitamins, and it adds a distinct bitter flavor to salads. Kale is a great base because it can stand up to moisture without weighing down the salad, and it can also be added to fresh pestos and stir-fry dishes. It is a tough, fibrous green that is typically "massaged" by tearing the leaves from the rib, placing them in a bowl or resealable bag, mixing in a bit of dressing, and gently massaging the leaves to soften them. This relaxes the kale and makes it a pleasant base for salads.

Mizuna greens. Also called Japanese mustard greens, these are milder in flavor and less peppery than arugula. They are dark green and have serrated edges. For the purposes of this book, they are essentially the same as mustard greens. Mizuna greens can be found in stores like Sprouts Farmers Market and Whole Foods. Many farmers' markets sell them, too.

Mustard greens. These are bitter greens with a distinct mustard or horseradish flavor. They are often used in East Asian, South Asian, and African cuisines. These greens are frequently pickled or fermented.

Parsley. Although mainly known as an herb or garnish, parsley is used as a base in some salads like tabouleh. It's slightly peppery and comes in two main varieties: Italian flat-leaf and curly. It adds freshness and earthiness to salads.

Radicchio/Italian chicory. This is a fantastic way to add bright purple or pink color to any salad. Radicchio has white "veins" running through it for an even more aesthetically pleasing natural component. It is often grilled and can also withstand bold flavorings and moisture without getting soggy. I don't use radicchio in any of the recipes in this book, but it's included in many mixes, so it's important to be familiar with it.

Romaine lettuce. This common salad green is the base of the famous Caesar salad and is commonly used in Middle Eastern cuisine. It has a mild flavor and is available year-round. It is crunchy and leafy, and it varies in color.

GRAINS

Bulgur wheat. Often referred to as cracked durum wheat, bulgur wheat is commonly found in Mediterranean and Middle Eastern cuisines. It is the base for tabouleh salad and is found in a variety of Mediterranean meze (appetizers) and soups. It is easily available at most large supermarkets and health food stores.

Couscous. Food so nice they named it twice! Somewhere between a grain and a pasta, couscous is mainly found in North African and Middle Eastern dishes. The traditional North African variety looks like tiny particles, whereas the Israeli pearl variety (called *ptitim* in Israel) looks like miniature spheres. Couscous also comes in the whole-wheat form for additional fiber content.

Farro. This is a nutty, rich grain that adds a ton of texture and bite to salads and grain bowls, and it is also used in soups. Farro packs a significant amount of protein, fiber, and whole grains, more than rice or quinoa. The only downside is that it's not gluten-free.

Pasta. Traditionally made from wheat, pasta comes in a variety of shapes and sizes. Nowadays you can find it made from lentils, brown rice, pumpkin, and more. Shapes like rotini are better for absorbing dressings. Pasta is a fantastic blank canvas for salads and can be used in all cuisines, not just the Italian dishes that it's known for.

Quinoa. This is a gluten-free seed (technically not a grain) native to Latin America that has a higher protein content than most grains. It is often used as a substitute for traditional wheat grains and has gained traction in the mainstream market as a healthy addition to salads and grain bowls.

Rice, brown. This healthier alternative to white rice packs a ton of fiber and adds a unique bite to any salad. The downside: It takes longer to cook than its white rice cousin. But the flavor, texture, and nutrition boost make it worth it.

Rice, forbidden. This rice is black in color and is often consumed in East Asian and South Asian regions. It has more fiber than brown rice and is frequently used in East Asian desserts and puddings. Forbidden rice is becoming more common and is carried by most large supermarket chains as well as organic groceries.

Rice, jasmine or basmati. Often used in Middle Eastern or South Asian cooking, this long-grain rice is aromatic and pairs well with lentils and spices.

Rice, long-grain. This is a less-starchy rice variety. It is mainly found in Middle Eastern pilafs and South Asian dishes.

Rice, short-grain. This type of rice is starchy, soft, and sticky. It makes perfect sushi rice and is a staple of Asian cooking as well as risottos and paella because it absorbs aromatics well.

Rice, wild. This rice packs a ton of nutrition and adds a contrast in texture and color to any salad. It is slightly chewy and crunchy at the same time, and is one of the healthier grain alternatives.

The Veggie or Fruit

The next components of the salad are fresh vegetables and fruits. They help balance out the flavors, contribute to texture, and add nutrition and fiber that help you feel satisfied and stay fuller longer naturally.

Bell peppers. Red, green, yellow, orange: The more colors you use, the merrier your salad. Each bell pepper adds a different level of sweetness—the further you go from green, the sweeter—but all add crunch and vibrant color.

Broccoli. One of the healthiest veggies on earth, broccoli can be baked, roasted, steamed, boiled, or fried.

Brussels sprouts. These miniature cabbages are a truly versatile power food. Roasted, pan-fried, baked, boiled, or steamed, they add a nice chewy texture and earthy tone to salads.

Butternut squash/pumpkin. Filled with beta carotene, veggies in this family taste like fall and add an earthy, naturally sweet flavor. They are wonderfully hearty, too.

Carrots. Shaved, shredded, or sliced, this household staple adds bright-orange color, crunch, and nutrition to any salad.

Cauliflower. Similar to broccoli, cauliflower can be prepared in a variety of ways. It also comes in a beautiful purple-hue variety. Nowadays, cauliflower is used as a substitute for rice. Called "cauliflower rice," it is pulsed in a food processor to look like rice and then pan-seared. It is a gluten-free, more easily digestible addition to salads.

Citrus fruits. These make fantastic sweet additions to salads with seafood or fattier cuts of meat. Citrus is also a great acidic component for salad dressings (discussed in the next chapter). Oranges, grapefruit, and clementines are welcome additions to any salad.

Cucumbers. Mild and refreshing, cucumbers are an excellent way to lighten up salads and provide a satisfying crunch. They pair incredibly well with chili powder and can also be made into quick pickles.

Peaches. When in season, peaches make the best addition to steak and leafy greens, in my opinion. They have the perfect texture and bite to them and the right amount of sugar that goes well with the fatty richness of steak. That, combined with the freshness of greens, makes for a very well-balanced and complex flavor and texture combination.

Radishes. These bitter, crispy, and refreshing root vegetables are found frequently in Mexican and Eastern European cuisines and add an amazing crunchy component to salads. The watermelon variety (pink on the inside, green on the outside) adds a ton of color and deeper flavor than the typical pink-rimmed radish.

Strawberries. Strawberries add a massive amount of fiber to salads and help texturally balance out leafier, crunchier, and richer components. Their natural sweetness provides an unexpected and welcome flavor to many salads.

Tomatoes. Is it a fruit, or is it a vegetable? I won't go into the semantics, but tomatoes in all their varieties—cherry, grape, on the vine, heirloom, and green—add sweetness, color, richness, and umami to salads.

Watermelon. Little else is as refreshing as a slice of cold, fresh watermelon on a warm summer night. When watermelon is in season, it is divine with salty cheeses such as cotija, feta, or halloumi (typically found in Middle Eastern cuisine). Watermelon adds natural sugar and sweetness.

The Protein

The third component of the salad is protein. Like fruits and veggies, proteins help keep you fuller longer and typically provide additional healthy lean fats that are necessary for cardio-vascular health.

Bacon. Bacon in a salad is a win in my book. It has the reputation of being an indulgent ingredient, but it can be eaten readily as part of a healthy diet. Try turkey bacon, pork bacon, or bacon labeled with a lower fat percentage.

Canned tuna. This must-have kitchen staple is a quick way to add lean protein to any salad. Make sure to buy the variety of tuna packed in water (instead of packed in oil) to control the fat content of your meals.

Chicken. This is the go-to protein. White meat (typically chicken breast) is the leanest option. Dark meat (chicken thigh) is a fattier option that is still a natural, healthy source of protein. Remember that the skin of the chicken is where most of the cholesterol is located. The skin helps the chicken stay moist, so remove it after cooking for a healthier alternative (if you have that kind of willpower!).

Cod. This flaky white fish is affordable and is a neutral protein addition to salads or bowls. Its mild flavor complements the stronger flavors of the greens or veggies you use.

Eggs. They are the world's cheapest and most readily accessible protein, and a personal favorite of mine. Soft-boiled, hard-boiled, and poached eggs are easy to make and are found in many of the recipes within this book.

Flank steak. This is an affordable, common cut of beef that cooks quickly and pairs well with most marinades, stone fruit, citrus fruit, and leafy greens.

Prosciutto. This sultry cured pork is salty, fatty, and rich. It pairs beautifully with crisp, sweet apples, asparagus—or pretty much anything.

Salmon. There's nothing like perfectly seared salmon with crispy skin. Ubiquitously eaten, it can be flavored and adapted for every type of world cuisine. It is an extremely lean protein packed with healthy fats, and is also environmentally sustainable.

Shrimp. This freezer-friendly crustacean is a lean source of protein that is a great addition to salads. Although high in cholesterol, it is arguably still one of the healthier forms of seafood.

Tofu. The soy-based fermented product, often used in Asian cooking. It comes in soft, firm, or extra-firm varieties, and can be marinated, baked, or fried. It will take on the flavor of any dressing, enhancing the flavor of your salad.

The Topping

Next up is the topping. This is an opportunity to really build on the textures and enrich the flavor profile of your salad.

Bacon bits. Can you really ever go wrong with bacon? Bacon bits add a nice salty, crunchy contrast to healthier salad bases and pack additional protein.

Cheese. Shredded Cheddar, fresh mozzarella, feta, halloumi, cotija, queso fresco, ricotta salata, and Parmesan are all used frequently in the recipes in this book. Although high in fat, cheese still provides healthy, complete proteins and welcome calcium.

Dried fruits. Dried cranberries and cherries are the most common additions to salads. They have a long shelf life and are great to keep in your pantry.

Nuts. Walnuts, pecans, hazelnuts, peanuts, almonds, and macadamias are all *nutritious* additions to salads. They add crunch and, well, nuttiness.

Seeds. Pumpkin seeds (pepitas), sunflower seeds, sesame seeds, and flaxseed are packed with protein and vitamins. They add healthy fats, nutrition, and a crunchy texture to salads. They have a long shelf life and will keep well in your pantry.

The Bonus

Last, but definitely not least, comes the bonus component of the salad. This is your time to shine and to customize your salad. Whether you're looking for a lighter salad or you don't have all the ingredients the recipe calls for, the bonus item allows for full flexibility and customization to your tastes, preferences, dietary needs, and cravings.

Obsessed with a specific ingredient in the recipe? Are you a cheese lover? Add an extra kind of cheese.

Not in the mood for meat or fish? Go vegetarian (or vegan)! Add an additional fruit or vegetable to replace the meat or fish item in a recipe.

Looking for more protein? Add an extra egg, double down on the serving of meat or fish, or add extra tofu.

What if I added this to my salad? Go wild! Roasted vegetables left over from last night's dinner? They are fantastic added to the next night's salad. Blackberries and red onions (raw or pickled) add an unexpected burst of flavor.

Have a new favorite spice? Sprinkle a small pinch of it over your salad if the ingredients you use are a natural pairing with that spice. You can create a new masterpiece.

ABOUT THE RECIPES

The recipes generally contain five primary ingredients: the base, veggie or fruit, protein, topping, and bonus. The dressing and some pantry staples and simple spices make up the rest of the recipe (those ingredients are noted in the next chapter). With your salad formula in place, the dressing and staple items bring your salad together into a delicious, filling dinner.

Not every salad will have all five components of the formula. Some components can serve as more than one part of the formula. While the cabbage slaw makes the base for the katsu in the Katsu Salad with Pickled Purple Cabbage and Carrots, the cabbage also serves as the vegetable. That's all to say that even though successful dinner salads won't always follow the full formula, you can still make hearty, satisfying dinner salads that everyone will enjoy.

PUTTING IT ALL TOGETHER

A salad made of ingredients on the bitter spectrum is not likely to be a successful creation; nor will a salad made up of a single texture be all that exciting. But there are several things you can keep in mind as you make your dinner salads that will transform them from "Really? A salad for dinner?" to "Why didn't we think of this sooner?"

It's All About the Flavor

Sweet, sour, salty, bitter, spicy. Multiple flavor profiles will elevate your dinner salad every time. And it's all about finding the right balance. The bitter, peppery flavor of arugula is a wonderful contrast to the sweetness of strawberries. Each recipe in the book includes a range of flavor profiles, all of which complement the ingredients in the salad. It's also about finding the right balance for your tastes. You may want a little extra of an ingredient because its spicy flavor profile is a real zing for your taste buds, or a little less of another ingredient because you find that it overpowers the other ingredients.

It's Crunch Time

The most successful dinner salad will be one that has varying textures. The crisp bite of carrots is a nice contrast to soft and creamy tofu. The chew of brown rice is balanced by the soft texture of baby spinach. You may have to vary the proportions to find your ideal balance, but you'll appreciate those contrasts every time.

For Every Salad There Is a Season

To state the obvious, some salad ingredients—vegetables and fruits in particular—are better at certain times of the year than others. Just think of the difference between an August tomato picked from the garden or farmer's stand and one from the supermarket in February. It's like night and day. Create your dinner salads around what's in season. Highlight that freshly picked August tomato, or enjoy the comfort of butternut squash in the chill of winter.

A Feast for the Eyes

The presentation of your salad is important. After all, we eat with our eyes first. How you build your plate (and ultimately serve it) is what first perks up your taste buds. Build your salad with a variety of colors. A salad of greens, cucumber, green bell pepper, and grilled chicken may taste delicious, but it looks boring on the plate. There's too much colorful bounty out there to keep everything monochromatic.

The Great Finish

How you season your salad can make the difference between good and great. Most salads will benefit from a little salt, lemon or lime juice, and vinegar. The citrus juice and vinegar may come from the dressing you use. Some of the ingredients you use in your salad—the protein, roasted vegetables, nuts, etc.—may already be salted. Nevertheless, it's important to taste the salad before serving it. An extra sprinkle of salt can turn it from "meh" to "wow!"

BASIC TECHNIQUES

When many people think of salads, they think only of raw fruits and vegetables. An amazing, delicious, and inspiring salad involves some basic cooking, roasting, pickling, toasting, searing, and poaching. The following are basic techniques for preparing certain ingredients you will use in your dinner salads. Even better, many can be prepped ahead of time so you have them on hand to put together your creations during the busy week ahead.

Roast Brussels sprouts. Preheat the oven to 375°F. Trim the Brussels sprouts and cut each in half lengthwise. Transfer to a baking sheet. Drizzle them with extra-virgin olive oil and season with salt and freshly ground black pepper. Toss to combine. Roast for 35 minutes, tossing the Brussels sprouts twice while they roast.

Roast butternut squash. Preheat the oven to 400°F. Peel and seed the butternut squash, then cut into cubes. Transfer to a baking sheet or large casserole dish. Drizzle the squash with extra-virgin olive oil and crushed garlic, and toss to combine. Roast for 25 to 30 minutes, or until fork tender.

Roast whole pumpkins. Preheat the oven to 350°F. Place the whole pumpkin on a baking sheet and roast for 50 to 60 minutes, or until the outside is soft. Cut the pumpkin in half. Scoop out the seeds and place them in a bowl (you can toast them later and use as a snack or a garnish for your salads). Scoop out the cooked pumpkin into a separate bowl.

Pickle red onion. Cut 1 large red onion into thin circles. Bring a small saucepan of water to a boil. While waiting for the water to boil, in a Mason jar, combine ¾ cup of rice wine vinegar, ½ teaspoon of white sugar, and ½ teaspoon of salt. If you like, you can also add other seasonings like garlic or peppercorns. Drop the sliced red onion into the boiling water for 30 seconds, then drain and pat dry. Place the onion in the jar with the vinegar mixture. Secure the lid on the jar and refrigerate for at least 30 minutes or, ideally, up to 4 hours before serving.

Cook quinoa. Quinoa is prepared using a 1-to-2 ratio of quinoa to liquid (1 cup quinoa to 2 cups water or broth, for example). Rinse the quinoa in a fine-mesh strainer under cold water, then drain. Place in a medium saucepan. Add the water or broth and a generous pinch of salt. Bring to a rolling boil, then reduce the heat to low, cover the pan, and cook for 15 to 20 minutes, or until all the liquid is absorbed. Remove the pan from the heat and fluff the quinoa with a fork.

Cook couscous. Couscous is prepared using a 1-to-1½ ratio of couscous to liquid (1 cup couscous to 1½ cups water or broth, for example). Bring a medium saucepan of water or broth to a boil. Add 1 tablespoon of butter or extra-virgin olive oil (optional) for ideal results. Stir in the couscous, remove the pan from the heat, and cover. Let sit for 10 minutes, or until all the liquid is absorbed. Remove the lid and fluff the couscous with a fork.

Cook rice noodles. Place rice noodles in a large heat-proof glass bowl. Pour boiling water over the noodles until they are fully submerged. After a few minutes, test the noodles to see if they are tender. Once tender, drain the noodles and run them under cold water. Toss with a small drizzle of sesame oil or other neutral oil to prevent the noodles from sticking together.

Cook bulgur wheat. Bulgur wheat is prepared using a 1-to-2 ratio of bulgur to liquid (1 cup bulgur to 2 cups water, for example). Place the bulgur in a large saucepan. Pour in the appropriate amount of boiling water. Cover the pan with a lid and let the bulgur sit for 25 to 30 minutes, or until all of the water has been absorbed. Fluff the bulgur with a fork.

Cook farro. Farro is prepared using a 1-to-2 ratio of farro to water (1 cup farro to 2 cups water, for example). Combine the farro and water in a large pot. Bring to a boil, then reduce the heat to low. Cover the pot and simmer for 25 to 30 minutes, or until all the water is absorbed.

Cook rice. Brown rice, white rice, and forbidden rice are prepared using a 1-to-2 ratio of rice to liquid (1 cup of rice to 2 cups water, for example). Wild rice is prepared using a 1-to-3 ratio of rice to liquid. Combine the rice and water in a large pot. Bring to a boil, then reduce the heat to low, cover the pot, and simmer until all the water is absorbed, about 20 minutes. White rice generally takes less time to cook, and wild rice may take longer. Fluff the cooked rice with a fork.

Cook lentils. Lentils are prepared using a 1-to-2 ratio of lentils to liquid (1 cup of lentils to 2 cups water, for example). Place the lentils in a fine-mesh strainer and rinse under cold water. Transfer the rinsed lentils to a medium saucepan and add water and, if desired, spices such as garlic cloves, bay leaves, and peppercorns. Bring to a simmer over medium-high heat, then reduce the heat to a gentle simmer. Cook the lentils, uncovered, for 20 to 30 minutes, adding water as necessary to ensure that they don't dry out. Remove the pan from the heat and season the lentils with salt.

Soft-boil eggs. Bring a saucepan filled with water to a rolling boil. Add a teaspoon of vinegar (to help with peeling the eggshells). Using either a large spoon or a ladle, gently add whole eggs to the water. Cook, uncovered, for 6 to 8 minutes on high heat. The cooking time depends on how runny you prefer your eggs and how many eggs you are cooking at a time. The more eggs you are cooking, the more likely you will need the full 8 minutes. To make sure that the eggs remain soft and the yolks runny, transfer the cooked eggs to a large bowl of ice water. Let chill for 2 minutes to stop the cooking process. Carefully peel the eggs and serve immediately.

Hard-boil eggs. Add whole eggs to a large saucepan and fill the pan with water. Add a teaspoon of vinegar (to help with peeling the eggshells). Place the pan over high heat and bring the water to a rolling boil. Cover the pan and remove it from the heat. Let the eggs sit for 10 minutes. To keep them from overcooking and turning gray inside, transfer the cooked eggs directly to a large bowl of ice water. Let chill for 2 minutes to stop the cooking process. Peel.

Poach eggs. In a large saucepan over medium-high heat, combine 2 to 3 inches of water and 1 teaspoon of vinegar and heat until small bubbles form. Crack 2 large eggs into 2 separate small bowls or ramekins and gently pour each egg into the hot water. Alternatively, crack an egg into a ladle and submerge it into the hot water; repeat for the second egg. Reduce the heat to medium and poach the eggs for 4 to 5 minutes, or until the whites are firm and opaque but the yolks are still runny.

Pan-sear salmon. Season both sides of a salmon fillet generously with salt and freshly ground black pepper. Place a large skillet over medium-high heat and drizzle it with extra-virgin olive oil, grapeseed oil, or other neutral oil. Once the oil is hot, add the salmon skin-side down. Sear until golden brown on the bottom and the skin becomes crispy, about 4 minutes. Gently flip the salmon with tongs and reduce the heat to medium. Cook the salmon for 3 to 4 minutes longer, or until it reaches your preferred level of doneness.

Tenderize and pan-fry chicken. With a meat tenderizer, pound the chicken breast until it is about ½ to ¾ inch thick. Season both sides of the breast generously with salt and freshly ground black pepper. Heat a drizzle of extra-virgin olive oil in a large skillet over high heat. Add the chicken and sear, about 2 minutes on each side. Cover the skillet, reduce the heat to medium-high, and continue cooking the chicken for about 10 minutes. Remove the lid, increase the heat to high, and cook the chicken for another 1 minute on each side.

Marinate and cook steak without a grill. Preheat the oven to 375°F. In a resealable bag, combine extra-virgin olive oil, minced garlic, rosemary, and flank steak. Seal the bag and massage the meat to cover it in the marinade. Let the steak marinate for 15 minutes. Remove the steak from the marinade (discarding the liquid) and season both sides generously with salt and freshly ground black pepper. Heat a large oven-safe skillet over high heat. Add the steak and sear on both sides, about 2 minutes per side. Transfer the skillet to the oven and continue cooking the steak for 10 minutes. Remove the skillet from the oven and place back on the stove over medium-high heat. Add 1 tablespoon of unsalted butter to the skillet to melt. Using a spoon, baste the steak with the melted butter for 2 minutes. Remove the skillet from the heat, cover with aluminum foil, and let the steak rest for 5 minutes before slicing against the grain into strips.

Toast nuts and sesame seeds. In a dry skillet over medium-high heat, spread the nuts or seeds in a single layer. Toast for 2 to 5 minutes, shaking the pan or stirring so the nuts or seeds don't burn. Transfer to a plate or bowl once toasted.

Your salad is all about the Base + Veggie/Fruit + Protein + Topping + Bonus. With those in place, all you need now is to finish it off with a drizzle of the perfect dressing.

CHAPTER 2

THE DRESSING FORMULA

You've learned all the components that make a foolproof salad—but to really take it to the next level, you need to know how to dress it all up. Just as salads can be made according to a formula, dressings are no different. Make some dressings ahead and store them for easy weeknight dinner salads. With great, simple-to-make, homemade dressings in your repertoire, you'll never go back to store-bought. Some dressings are dairy-based and creamy, and typically don't last more than a few days, while others are oil- or vinegar-based and can last for weeks.

THE DRESSING FORMULA

The perfect salad dressing can be divided into a few main components and, just like the salad formula, is simple arithmetic.

Base B
+
Acid A
+
Emulsifier E
+
Seasoning S
+
Aromatics A
=
The Perfect, Foolproof Dressing

A simple rule-of-thumb ratio for base ingredients to acidic ingredients is typically 3 to 1. Begin with this baseline ratio and, depending on your taste preferences, you can adjust accordingly.

The Dressing Base

Let's begin with the base, which is the building block of your dressing.

Avocado. Avocado-based dressings are gaining popularity because of their high fiber content and creamy texture.

Cultured Buttermilk. Buttermilk is a creamy fermented-cow's-milk product that is sour from the addition of bacteria. The dairy component makes it a fantastic partner for spicy dressing ingredients. Buttermilk is great for tenderizing salads and adding a lot of moisture.

Mayonnaise. For rich, creamy dressings, mayonnaise is a great blank canvas and base for additional ingredients. Mix with sour cream to create a tart balance.

Oil. Extra-virgin olive oil is the most frequently used salad dressing, but don't neglect the other fantastic oils out there. Grapeseed, canola, avocado, and vegetable are all neutral oils that combine well with virtually all ingredients. For Asian-inspired dressings, sesame and coconut oils pack a ton of flavor and pair well with other Asian ingredients such as ginger and citrus. For Latin-inspired dressings, corn and sunflower oils help add flavor true to the region.

Tahini. Tahini is a paste made of crushed sesame seeds. Often consumed in the Middle East, it is a good base for Asian dressings as well.

Yogurt. Yogurt has made its way into many modern salad dressings because it is a healthier substitute for other bases that are typically higher in fat. Yogurt is also rich in protein and has digestion-boosting probiotics, making it a preferred salad dressing base for health-conscious people. For maximum protein and health benefits, use Greek yogurt.

The Acid

After the base, comes the acidic component of the dressing. This comes in many different forms and can be adjusted to your tastes and preferences.

Apple cider vinegar. This vinegar, made, as the name suggests, from apples, is very intense in flavor. It's commonly used as a health food for its tremendous nutritional benefits, and is also often used in salad dressings and for pickling.

Balsamic vinegar. This is a dark, concentrated vinegar made from grape must, the remnants of a grape after it is squeezed. It packs an intense flavor, so be careful when using it in dressings. A little can go a long way.

Citrus fruits. Citrus is a great way to add not only acid but also natural sugars to a dressing. Lemons, limes, grapefruits, oranges, kumquats, and other citrus fruits make fantastic additions to dressings.

Distilled white vinegar. This is the most inexpensive vinegar available. It has a very potent smell and is produced by fermenting ethanol and bacteria. If using distilled white vinegar, you'll need some trial and error to find the right balance for your tastes. It is also used for pickling.

Rice vinegar. Rice vinegar is one of the more neutral, mild vinegars used as an acid in salad dressings. It is made from fermented rice and is most common in Asian cuisine.

White wine vinegar. This vinegar is mild in flavor and packs a subtle fruity flavor. It pairs fantastically with Mediterranean cuisines.

The Emulsifier

After the acid comes the emulsifier component of the dressing. This comes in many different forms and acts as a binding agent for the rest of the ingredients in the dressing.

Avocado. Avocado can be used as either the base or emulsifier component of salad dressings—sometimes serving as both. Its fat content and creamy and smooth texture are a great addition.

Egg yolks. Eggs are wildly versatile, and using the yolks in salad dressings is no exception. The yolk is packed with fat and vitamins, which lend a ton of flavor to dressings.

Mayonnaise. Like avocado, mayonnaise can be used as either the base or emulsifier component of salad dressings. Its mild taste is a great vehicle and blank canvas that pairs well with most flavorings.

Mustard. Mustard is a common condiment, but it's also an extremely flavorful addition to any salad dressing. Whether you use honey mustard, Dijon mustard, yellow mustard, or whole-grain mustard, it's a powerful dressing component.

The Seasoning

The fourth part of the dressing formula is the seasoning component. This comes in many different forms and adds a distinct flavor profile.

Honey. Honey is a natural sweetener that not only adds a distinct flavor to the dressing but also helps balance its acidic or spicy components.

Soy sauce. Soy sauce is a great way to add a ton of flavor without many calories. Choose the reduced-sodium kind to control the sodium level of your salads.

Spices. Spices such as cumin, paprika, chili powder, cayenne pepper, curry powder, Tajín, za'atar, salt, and freshly ground black pepper help flavor dressings and are calorie-free.

The Aromatics

The aromatics are the final component of the dressing formula. These come in many different forms and add an inviting, alluring aroma to any dressing.

Chiles. Adding fresh chiles, such as jalapeños, habaneros, or ghost peppers (if you're feeling really bold), gives an intense flavor to any salad dressing and a welcome hit of heat.

Garlic. Fresh garlic cloves add a discrete, vibrant bouquet to any dressing. For maximum impact, crush the garlic a bit with your hands or the flat side of a knife to release its natural aroma.

Ginger, lemongrass, or wasabi. Freshly grated ginger or lemongrass, or wasabi paste or powder, adds a bright aroma and depth of flavor to any dressing. Used mainly in Asian cuisines, these ingredients have tremendous health benefits as well. Ginger is an anti-inflammatory and it improves digestion, reduces nausea, and helps fight colds and flu. Lemongrass is a natural pain reliever and helps fight colds and flu. Wasabi is also an anti-inflammatory and has properties to prevent cancer. All three are full of antioxidants.

Herbs. Herbs such as parsley, cilantro, mint, sage, rosemary, thyme, oregano, basil, and dill add an earthy, fresh component to salad dressings. If using dry herbs, make sure first to rub them with your hands to release their natural oils and flavors.

ABOUT THE DRESSING RECIPES

Super-flavorful dressings can be achieved without all five of the dressing-formula components. A basic vinaigrette like the Lemon Vinaigrette (page 146) does not contain an emulsifier. That doesn't mean it's not a great dressing to give the perfect finishing touch to your dinner salad. After all, sometimes the best things are the simplest.

I typically use about 2 tablespoons of dressing per salad serving. Those are the amounts I've included with each recipe. If you prefer a lighter or heavier touch to the dressing on your salad, you can, of course, adjust the amount accordingly.

BASIC INGREDIENTS

Stock your refrigerator, pantry, and spice rack with the following items. These pantry staples and spices will quickly become part of your well-stocked kitchen, if they aren't already included.

Fridge Staples

- Butter (unsalted)
- Lime and lemon juice
- Mayonnaise
- Miso paste
- Mustard (Dijon, honey, and whole-grain)
- Pickles
- Sour cream
- Tahini
- Yogurt

Pantry Staples

- All-purpose flour
- Balsamic vinegar
- Beans (black and kidney)
- Bread crumbs (Italian and panko)
- Canola oil
- Chickpeas
- Croutons
- Extra-virgin olive oil
- Grapeseed oil
- Honey
- Lentils
- Rice noodles
- Rice vinegar
- Sesame oil
- Soy sauce
- Sugar (brown and granulated)
- Tortilla chips
- White wine vinegar

Spice Rack Staples

- Cayenne pepper
- Chili powder
- Cumin
- Curry powder
- Garlic powder
- Ground cinnamon
- Ground ginger
- Jerk seasoning
- Paprika
- Pepper (freshly ground black or multicolored peppercorns add the most flavor)
- Red pepper flakes
- Rosemary
- Salt (sea salt, Himalayan pink salt, black salt, and kosher salt are all "healthier" salts since they include more minerals)
- Shawarma seasoning
- Tajín (This is chili powder with lime. It's incredibly flavorful and tangy, and has a bit of a kick. It can be substituted with traditional chili powder mixed with fresh lime juice or lime zest, but the real thing is worth a trip to the store or an online purchase.)

You've got your salad and dressing formulas down, and your pantry and spice rack are well stocked. Now it's time to make hearty, flavorful salads that will transform what you think is possible for a satisfying dinner.

PART II
THE RECIPES

The chapters that follow include recipes for salads that are hearty, satisfying, and easy to make for dinner. All the recipes utilize the salad formula for success: Base + Veggie/Fruit + Protein + Topping + Bonus. Dressing recipes are in the final chapter and follow their own easy-to-remember formula: Base + Acid + Emulsifier + Seasoning + Aromatics. The recipes are inspired by flavors from around the world. Creating dinner salads utilizing global foods, spices, and flavors opens the door to exciting, lively, satisfying meals. Enjoy this journey from East to West, without leaving the comfort of your own home. We'll start in Asia, hop over to Europe, detour to the Middle East and the Mediterranean, make a pit stop in Latin America, and come home to the United States.

SALMON AND BRUSSELS SPROUT SALAD *page 40*

CHAPTER 3

ASIAN-INSPIRED SALADS

A sian food is characterized by rice, noodles, seafood, tons of veggies, and depending on the region, chiles. The dinner salad recipes in this chapter draw their inspiration from enticing Asian flavor combinations, like those found in my Vietnamese Spring Roll Salad (page 30) where rice noodles take the place of rice wrappers, my Hawaiian Poke Salad (page 37), which in itself represents the blend of Asian cultures combining in Hawaii, and South Asian flavors like those in my Indian Curried Lentil and Paneer Salad (page 43).

CRAB, ORANGE, CURLED SCALLION, AND EGG RICE SALAD

SERVES 4

PREP TIME: 30 MINUTES / FINISH TIME: 5 MINUTES / TOTAL TIME: 35 MINUTES

DAIRY-FREE

I've always loved imitation crab salads because they have a delicious, creamy flavor. The crab pairs perfectly with citrus and, of course, eggs. Furikake seasoning is a blend of dried seaweed and sesame seeds, and is a delicious garnish on rice. It can be found in the Asian section of most large grocery stores, at health food stores, or Asian specialty stores.

1 cup forbidden rice, brown rice, or sushi rice B
4 large eggs T
¼ teaspoon vinegar
2 oranges, peeled V
½ cup Asian Soy Vinaigrette (page 147)
3 large scallions, green parts only B
12 ounces imitation crab sticks P
Furikake seasoning, to garnish (optional)

1. Cook the rice according to the instructions on page 13.

2. Soft-boil the eggs with the vinegar according to the instructions on page 14. Peel and set aside until ready to plate.

3. While the rice and eggs cook, cut the oranges into wedges. Place in a large bowl and toss with the soy vinaigrette.

4. Cut the scallion greens into long, thin strips. Place the strips in a bowl of ice water. Let sit for 5 to 10 minutes.

5. Cut the crab sticks into bite-size pieces. Add to the bowl with the oranges and stir to combine.

6. Pick the curled scallions out of the ice water and gently pat dry with a paper towel. Add them to the crab-orange mixture and stir to combine.

7. Divide the warm rice among four plates, then top with the dressed crab-orange mixture. Cut each soft-boiled egg in half lengthwise, and place two halves on top of each salad. Garnish the salads with a sprinkle of furikake seasoning (if using). Serve warm.

TECHNIQUE TIP: Curling scallions is one of the easiest tricks in the kitchen—but the end result looks fancy and as if it takes a lot of time and effort. The secret to success is placing thin strips of scallion greens into ice-cold water to loosen the fibers. This naturally turns them into adorable ribbon-like curls, and also makes them extra crunchy.

SUBSTITUTION TIP: Substitute the crab with shrimp or chicken. For a vegetarian salad, use tofu for the protein.

PER SERVING

Calories: 353; Fat: 11g; Sodium: 2,248mg; Carbohydrates: 37g; Protein: 17g; Fiber: 3g

CHINESE MANDARIN CHICKEN SALAD

SERVES 4

PREP TIME: 30 MINUTES / FINISH TIME: 5 MINUTES / TOTAL TIME: 35 MINUTES

DAIRY-FREE

This Chinese chicken salad is far more American than it is Chinese, but its flavors are inspired by the Far East. The fried chow mein noodles provide a satisfying crunch to the dish. If you can't find the noodles in your grocery store, substitute them with white corn tortilla chips. Just gently crumble the chips before adding to the salad.

1 medium head green cabbage B
½ cup Cilantro-Lime Dressing (page 152)
1 pound chicken breast P
Salt
Freshly ground black pepper
½ teaspoon Chinese five-spice powder (optional)
1 tablespoon sesame oil
1 (11-ounce) can mandarin orange slices, drained and juice reserved V
1 cup slivered almonds T
1 cup fried chow mein noodles B

1. Halve the cabbage lengthwise and remove the core. Thinly slice the leaves. In a large bowl, toss the cabbage with the cilantro-lime dressing.

2. Tenderize the chicken by pounding the breast with a meat tenderizer. Cut into bite-size pieces and place in a medium bowl. Season the chicken generously with salt and pepper. Toss with the Chinese five-spice powder (if using).

3. In a large skillet, heat the sesame oil over high heat. Add the chicken and brown the pieces on all sides. Once browned, reduce the heat to medium and continue cooking the chicken, stirring occasionally, for about 10 minutes, or until cooked through. Remove the skillet from the heat.

4. While the chicken is cooking, stir 1 to 2 tablespoons of the reserved mandarin orange juice into the cabbage for an extra burst of citrus flavor. (Reserve the remaining juice to make salad dressings, or discard.) Add the mandarin orange slices to the cabbage and toss to combine.

5. In a small skillet, toast the almonds following the instructions on page 15.

6. Add the cooked chicken to the cabbage and oranges. Add the fried chow mein noodles and toss to combine. Divide the salad among four plates and top with the toasted almonds. Serve at room temperature or chilled.

INGREDIENT TIP: Think of fried chow mein noodles like Asian croutons. They are highly addictive, so beware! You can buy them at most Asian groceries and in the international aisle of the supermarket.

PER SERVING

Calories: 539; Fat: 39g; Sodium: 198mg; Carbohydrates: 18g; Protein: 32g; Fiber: 5g

VIETNAMESE SPRING ROLL SALAD

SERVES 4

PREP TIME: 20 MINUTES / FINISH TIME: 5 MINUTES / TOTAL TIME: 25 MINUTES

DAIRY-FREE

Fresh spring rolls are like little Asian burritos, with a ton of room for variability and experimentation. For me, the best Vietnamese spring rolls are the ones where you can taste both the individual ingredients and how they work together. It's the best of both worlds. This salad is a deconstructed version of a classic Vietnamese spring roll, packed with the same great flavors, that makes for a hearty dinner.

1 (8-ounce) package rice noodles **B**
1 tablespoon sesame oil
1 pound shrimp, peeled and deveined, or ground pork **P**
Salt
Freshly ground black pepper
2 tablespoons soy sauce (if making pork)
1½ cups loosely packed fresh mint leaves **T**
1 cup peanuts **B**
2 large carrots, cut into thin strips **V**
½ cup Ginger-Miso Vinaigrette (page 154)

1. Place the rice noodles in a large heat-proof glass bowl and prepare according to the instructions on page 13.

2. While the rice noodles soak, heat the sesame oil in a large skillet over medium-high heat. If making the shrimp, add them to the skillet and cook, turning occasionally, until they are pink on both sides, about 3 minutes. Transfer to a plate and season with salt and pepper. If making the pork, add the meat to the skillet with the hot sesame oil, using a wooden spoon to break it into crumbles. Drizzle the soy sauce over the pork and continue cooking until it is browned and cooked through, 5 to 8 minutes. Remove the skillet from the heat.

3. Tear the mint leaves into bite-size pieces.

4. In a medium skillet over high heat, toast the peanuts according to the instructions on page 15.

5. Add the shrimp or pork, the mint, carrots, and toasted peanuts to the bowl with the rice noodles. Toss with the ginger-miso vinaigrette. Serve warm.

SUBSTITUTION TIP: Want to go vegetarian? Use tofu as the protein. Season it with the soy sauce while it cooks.

PER SERVING

Calories: 812; Fat: 46g; Sodium: 508mg; Carbohydrates: 65g; Protein: 37g; Fiber: 10g

CHILLED MISO TOFU, CUCUMBER, AND RADISH SALAD

SERVES 3

PREP TIME: 30 MINUTES / FINISH TIME: 5 MINUTES / TOTAL TIME: 35 MINUTES

VEGETARIAN, NUT-FREE, DAIRY-FREE

This cold salad is loaded with fresh ingredients and packed with protein to keep you satisfied. The lightly pickled radish, carrot, and cucumber provide a delightful crunch to counterbalance the creaminess of the tofu. It's all rounded out with the umami flavors of the ginger-miso dressing.

3 large carrots V
1 tablespoon rice vinegar
2 Persian cucumbers V
2 large radishes V
1 pound firm tofu P
6 cups mizuna greens (Japanese mustard greens) B
6 tablespoons Ginger-Miso Vinaigrette (page 154)

1. Use a vegetable peeler to shave the carrots into ribbons. Place them in a large bowl and toss them with the vinegar.

2. Halve the cucumbers lengthwise, then remove the seeds by running a teaspoon across the flesh. Thinly cut the cucumbers into half-moons. Add them to the carrots and toss to combine.

3. Halve the radishes, then slice into half-moons as thinly as possible. Add them to the bowl with the carrots and cucumbers and toss to combine.

4. Cube the tofu and add it to the vegetables.

5. Add the mizuna greens to the bowl. Drizzle with the vinaigrette and toss to combine.

6. Refrigerate the salad for at least 15 minutes before serving. Serve cold.

SUBSTITUTION TIP: If mizuna greens aren't readily available, use a baby spring mix.

PER SERVING
Calories: 402; Fat: 29g; Sodium: 245mg; Carbohydrates: 25g; Protein: 17g; Fiber: 8g

KATSU SALAD WITH PICKLED PURPLE CABBAGE AND CARROTS

SERVES 2

PREP TIME: 30 MINUTES / FINISH TIME: 5 MINUTES / TOTAL TIME: 35 MINUTES

NUT-FREE

Asian fried chicken salad, need I say more? Well, I'm always happy to sing the praises of this salad. The slightly sour saltiness of the lightly pickled cabbage and carrots are wonderfully balanced by the flavor-packed katsu. The creaminess of the dressing brings it all together with just the right amount of zing. The salad doesn't have a topping or bonus component of the formula, but you can always top it with some slivered almonds and/or add some cotija or queso fresco for an Asian-Mexican fusion salad.

2 tablespoons rice vinegar

1 tablespoon soy sauce

1 tablespoon sesame oil

3 cups shredded purple cabbage B

3 large carrots, peeled and shaved V

2 medium chicken breasts
   (about ¾ pound total) P

¾ cup all-purpose flour

Salt

Freshly ground black pepper

1 egg

2 cups panko bread crumbs

Grapeseed, canola, or vegetable oil,
   for frying

¼ cup Creamy Chipotle Dressing
   (page 156)

1. Whisk together the rice vinegar, soy sauce, and sesame oil in a large bowl. Add the cabbage and carrots and toss to combine. Set aside, stirring occasionally while you prepare the rest of the salad, to let the vegetables pickle slightly.

2. Butterfly the chicken breasts (see Technique tip).

3. Place the flour on a large plate and season it with salt and pepper. In a medium bowl, beat the egg. Place the panko bread crumbs on another large plate. Line up the flour plate, the beaten egg, and the panko plate in a row.

4. Dredge one piece of the butterflied chicken in the seasoned flour, then dip it in the egg. Place the chicken on the plate with the panko bread crumbs and firmly press it down into the bread crumbs. Turn over and press the other side into the bread crumbs so the chicken is fully coated. Transfer to a plate and repeat the process with the second piece of butterflied chicken.

5. In a large skillet, heat a thin layer of oil over medium-high heat. Add one of the chicken pieces and cook until golden brown on both sides, about 5 minutes per side. Transfer the katsu chicken to a plate and repeat with the second piece of chicken. Alternatively, use two skillets to cook the chicken at the same time. Slice the chicken into thick strips.

6. Divide the cabbage and carrot mixture between two bowls. Add the katsu strips and drizzle with the dressing. Serve while the chicken is warm.

TECHNIQUE TIP: To butterfly a chicken breast, hold it down with your hand against a cutting board. With a very sharp knife, cut through the breast almost all the way. Open the breast (like a butterfly). This will yield a thin "sheet" of butterflied chicken breast. This creates a lot of surface area on the chicken and will make the katsu cook faster.

PER SERVING

Calories: 641; Fat: 18g; Sodium: 947mg; Carbohydrates: 66g; Protein: 52g; Fiber: 7g

RICE NOODLE SALAD WITH ORANGE AND EDAMAME

SERVES 2

PREP TIME: 30 MINUTES / FINISH TIME: 5 MINUTES / TOTAL TIME: 35 MINUTES

VEGETARIAN, DAIRY-FREE

Rice noodles combined with orange, edamame, and peanuts create a quick, easy, and healthy weeknight dinner solution. Edamame is a tasty and healthy snack, too. Bring a small container of them to work for mid-afternoon munching.

½ (8-ounce) package rice noodles B
2 large oranges V
1 cup peanuts B
1 cup shelled edamame beans P
¼ cup Ginger-Miso Vinaigrette (page 154)

1. Prepare the rice noodles according to the instructions on page 13.

2. While the rice noodles soak, peel the oranges and cut them into wedges.

3. Toast the peanuts in a medium skillet according to the instructions on page 15.

4. Place the rice noodles, orange wedges, and edamame in a large bowl. Toss with the vinaigrette.

5. Divide the salad between two plates. Garnish with the toasted peanuts. Serve warm or at room temperature.

INGREDIENT TIP: Frozen shelled edamame beans are a must-have item. They're packed with fiber and healthy fats, and make an easy and nutritious addition to almost any Asian-inspired salad. They can be thawed and eaten, or heated for a minute in a pot of salted water.

SUBSTITUTION TIP: Use egg noodles or vermicelli in place of the rice noodles.

PER SERVING

Calories: 968; Fat: 61g; Sodium: 258mg; Carbohydrates: 88g; Protein: 29g; Fiber: 14g

PICKLED CARROT, GRAPEFRUIT, AND SHRIMP SALAD

SERVES 3

PREP TIME: 15 MINUTES / FINISH TIME: 5 MINUTES / TOTAL TIME: 20 MINUTES

NUT-FREE, DAIRY-FREE

The tartness of fresh citrus combined with pickled carrots and fresh shrimp makes for a simple and flavorful Asian-inspired salad.

3 large carrots V
2 tablespoons rice vinegar
1 tablespoon soy sauce
2 tablespoons sesame oil, divided
1 grapefruit T
6 cups mizuna greens (Japanese mustard greens) B
1½ pounds shrimp, peeled and deveined P
6 tablespoons Charred Grapefruit Vinaigrette (page 160)

1. Use a vegetable peeler to shave the carrots into ribbons. Place them in a large bowl and toss with the vinegar, soy sauce, and 1 tablespoon of sesame oil. Set the bowl aside to let the carrots quick-pickle, stirring occasionally.

2. Peel the grapefruit and cut into wedges. Add to the bowl of carrots along with the mizuna greens and toss to combine.

3. In a large skillet, heat the remaining 1 tablespoon of sesame oil over high heat. When hot, add the shrimp and cook until pink and cooked through, about 2 minutes per side.

4. Add the shrimp to the bowl with the salad. Drizzle with the vinaigrette and toss to combine.

5. Divide the salad among three bowls. Serve at room temperature.

SUBSTITUTION TIP: Use baby spring mix in place of mizuna greens.

PER SERVING

Calories: 626; Fat: 38g; Sodium: 730mg; Carbohydrates: 18g; Protein: 50g; Fiber: 6g

FENNEL, SEARED PORK, AND PINEAPPLE SALAD

SERVES 4

PREP TIME: 30 MINUTES / FINISH TIME: 5 MINUTES / TOTAL TIME: 35 MINUTES

GLUTEN-FREE, NUT-FREE, DAIRY-FREE

You wouldn't know it to look at it, but fennel is part of the carrot family. Take a whiff of freshly cut fennel and you'll catch the aroma of black licorice. You'll taste only a hint of it when you eat it, though. Fennel pairs well with the tender meatiness of the pork here, and the pineapple is a sweet finish to this quick, satisfying salad.

1 pound pork tenderloin, trimmed, de-boned (or purchase already de-boned), and cut into 12 (¼-inch) slices P
Salt
Freshly ground black pepper
¼ cup grapeseed, vegetable, or canola oil
2 small fennel bulbs, fronds removed B
½ cup Date-Balsamic Vinaigrette (page 163)
½ small pineapple, diced (about 2 cups) V

1. Generously season the pork slices on both sides with salt and pepper.

2. Heat the oil in a large skillet over medium-high heat. When the oil is hot, add the pork slices in a single layer and sear them, about 3 minutes on each side. Cook in two batches, if necessary, or cook in two separate skillets to save time. Transfer the pork to a plate and let rest for 5 to 10 minutes.

3. While the pork rests, use a mandoline or very sharp knife to shave the fennel. Place it in a medium bowl and toss with the vinaigrette. Add the pineapple and toss to combine. Divide the fennel and pineapple among four bowls.

4. Slice the pork into thin strips. Top the salads with the pork strips and serve.

LEFTOVER TIP: Have extra pineapple from using a fresh one? Toss the leftover fruit into a blender with yogurt, bananas, and berries for a morning pick-me-up.

SUBSTITUTION TIP: Use baby spring mix in place of mizuna greens.

PER SERVING
Calories: 549; Fat: 34g; Sodium: 183mg; Carbohydrates: 44g; Protein: 27g; Fiber: 7g

HAWAIIAN POKE SALAD

SERVES 4

PREP TIME: 30 MINUTES / FINISH TIME: 5 MINUTES / TOTAL TIME: 35 MINUTES

NUT-FREE, DAIRY-FREE

Poke is a traditional Hawaiian dish. It's a blend of Asian flavors thanks to the many cultures that have landed on the islands. It is my go-to takeout dinner solution if I'm in a rush but still want to eat healthy. Poke tastes best made at home, because you can control the sodium levels and fully customize it to your taste.

1 cup brown rice **B**

¾ to 1 pound sashimi-grade ahi tuna **P**

8 tablespoons Asian Soy Vinaigrette (page 147), divided

3 cups mizuna greens (Japanese mustard greens) **V**

2 tablespoons minced chives **B**

2 small avocados, thinly sliced **T**

1. Place the rice and 2 cups of water in a large pot. Cook according to the instructions on page 14. Once cooked, cool down the rice by placing it in the refrigerator for 5 minutes.

2. While the rice cooks, prepare the other ingredients. Cut the tuna into bite-size cubes. Place it in a medium bowl and toss with 2 tablespoons of vinaigrette. Let the tuna sit and marinate for 15 to 20 minutes.

3. Place the mizuna greens in a large bowl and drizzle with the remaining 6 tablespoons of dressing. Toss to combine. Add the cooled rice and toss to combine.

4. Stir the chives into the tuna.

5. Divide the greens and rice among four bowls. Top with the marinated tuna and chives. Serve at room temperature, or refrigerate first to serve chilled. Just before serving, top with the avocado slices.

INGREDIENT TIP: Poke means "cut." There are as many varieties as there are people who make it. Fresh cubed pieces of raw fish are marinated in a jam-packed sauce and topped with ingredients like crab salad, avocado, wakame salad—you name it.

PER SERVING

Calories: 551; Fat: 27g; Sodium: 1,515mg; Carbohydrates: 51g; Protein: 12g; Fiber: 29g

TOMATO-RAMEN SALAD

SERVES 4

PREP TIME: 30 MINUTES / FINISH TIME: 5 MINUTES / TOTAL TIME: 35 MINUTES

VEGETARIAN, NUT-FREE, DAIRY-FREE

Little else is as comforting as a big bowl of hot, rich ramen soup on a cold winter night. I'm not talking about the college-favorite packaged variety, but rather the steaming bowls of noodles, vegetables, and protein found in many a restaurant. This ramen-inspired salad hits all the flavor notes of a bowl of ramen, with roasted tomatoes added for umami flavor.

1 (8-ounce) package rice noodles **B**

4 tablespoons sesame, grapeseed, canola, or vegetable oil, divided

12 ounces firm tofu, cubed **P**

2 cups cherry tomatoes, halved **V**

4 large scallions, greens parts only **T**

4 eggs **B**

½ cup Ginger-Miso Vinaigrette (page 154)

1. Preheat the broiler.

2. Prepare the rice noodles according to the instructions on page 13.

3. Heat 2 tablespoons of oil in a large skillet over medium-high heat. Once the oil is hot, add the tofu cubes and pan-fry them until golden brown on all sides, 1 to 2 minutes per side.

4. Place the tomato halves and the scallion greens on a rimmed baking sheet. Drizzle them with the remaining 2 tablespoons of oil and toss to coat. Arrange the tomato halves so they are cut-side down. Broil for about 5 minutes, or until the vegetables start to wilt and are slightly charred.

5. Roughly chop the broiled scallion greens.

6. While the tomatoes and scallions are roasting, soft-boil the eggs according to the instructions on page 14. Once chilled, peel the eggs.

7. Divide the rice noodles, tofu, tomatoes, and chopped scallions among four bowls. Top each with a soft-boiled egg and drizzle with the vinaigrette. Serve warm.

TECHNIQUE TIP: Roasted tomatoes add an umami flavor to almost anything. The roasting process caramelizes the natural sugars found in tomatoes and brings out their sweetness.

SUBSTITUTION TIP: Your stock of rice noodles out? Use egg noodles or vermicelli instead.

PER SERVING

Calories: 676; Fat: 44g; Sodium: 328mg; Carbohydrates: 57g; Protein: 16g; Fiber: 4g

ASIAN CUCUMBER SALAD WITH STEAK

SERVES 2

PREP TIME: 40 MINUTES / FINISH TIME: 5 MINUTES / TOTAL TIME: 45 MINUTES

Public service announcement: This salad is incredibly addictive. Cold, thinly sliced Persian cucumbers slightly pickled in an Asian vinaigrette with warm, decadent steak will be your new favorite. It's a great dinner to prepare for guests. They'll think you labored over the dish; instead, you've packed together a lot of great flavor in a short amount of time.

2 tablespoons sesame oil
1 garlic clove, minced
2 (4-ounce) flank steaks **P**
4 large Persian cucumbers **B**
¼ cup Asian Soy Vinaigrette (page 147)
Salt
Freshly ground black pepper
1 tablespoon unsalted butter
3 tablespoons sesame seeds **T**
2 tablespoons soy sauce
½ teaspoon red pepper flakes
  (optional) **B**

1. Preheat the oven to 375°F.

2. In a resealable bag, combine the sesame oil, minced garlic, and flank steaks. Seal the bag and massage the meat to coat it in the marinade. Set aside and let marinate for 15 minutes.

3. While the steak marinates, thinly slice the cucumbers. Place them in a small bowl and toss with the vinaigrette. Refrigerate and let marinate until ready to serve.

4. Remove the steaks from the marinade (discarding the liquid) and season generously on both sides with salt and pepper. Place a large oven-safe skillet over high heat. Once very hot, add the steaks and sear on both sides, about 2 minutes per side. Transfer the skillet to the oven and continue cooking the steaks for 10 minutes.

5. Remove the skillet from the oven and place back on the stove over medium-high heat. Add the butter to melt. Using a spoon, baste the steaks with the melted butter for 2 minutes. Remove the skillet from the heat and loosely cover with aluminum foil. Let the steaks rest for 5 minutes.

6. While the steak rests, lightly toast the sesame seeds in a small skillet according to the instructions on page 15.

7. Slice the steak against the grain into strips.

8. Divide the cucumbers between two bowls and top with the steak strips and toasted sesame seeds. Garnish the salad with the soy sauce and red pepper flakes (if using).

MAKE-AHEAD TIP: The cucumber salad tastes best after a few hours or even a day of marinating.

PER SERVING
Calories: 638; Fat: 57g; Sodium: 2,570mg; Carbohydrates: 31g; Protein: 33g; Fiber: 5g

SALMON AND BRUSSELS SPROUT SALAD

SERVES 2

PREP TIME: 40 MINUTES / FINISH TIME: 5 MINUTES / TOTAL TIME: 45 MINUTES

DAIRY-FREE

Salmon and Brussels sprouts may not seem like a natural combination, but they are a perfect balance of protein and fiber without sacrificing flavor. The heartiness of the Brussels sprouts complements the milder flavor of the salmon. And when served with quinoa, you're getting a one-two protein punch, guaranteed to leave you satiated.

2 cups Brussels sprouts V
1 large red bell pepper, thinly sliced B
¼ cup sesame oil
Salt
Freshly ground black pepper
¾ cup quinoa B
2 (4- to 5-ounce) salmon fillets P
Extra-virgin olive oil, for rubbing
3 tablespoons sesame seeds, lightly toasted T
¼ cup Asian Soy Vinaigrette (page 147)
½ teaspoon red pepper flakes (optional)

1. Preheat the oven to 375°F.

2. Trim the Brussels sprouts and halve them lengthwise. Place on a baking sheet along with the bell pepper. Drizzle the vegetables with the sesame oil and season with salt and pepper. Toss to combine and coat the vegetables. Roast for 35 minutes, tossing the vegetables twice.

3. Cook the quinoa according to the instructions on page 13.

4. Rub the salmon fillets generously with olive oil, then season on both sides with salt and pepper. Pan-sear the salmon according to the instructions on page 15. Once cooked, transfer the salmon to a plate and flake with a fork.

5. In a small skillet, lightly toast the sesame seeds according to the instructions on page 15.

6. Divide the quinoa, Brussels sprouts, and bell pepper between two bowls. Top with the flaked salmon and drizzle with the vinaigrette. Garnish the salads with the toasted sesame seeds and red pepper flakes (if using). Serve warm.

MAKE-AHEAD TIP: This salad is perfect for meal prepping because of its simple components. Make the quinoa in bulk, sear (or bake) a few salmon fillets, and roast double the amount of Brussels sprouts in one go. The vinaigrette can be made in advance and stored for weeks in the refrigerator.

PER SERVING

Calories: 868; Fat: 53g; Sodium: 1,620mg; Carbohydrates: 61g; Protein: 41g; Fiber: 10g

CITRUS AND SEARED AHI TUNA SALAD

SERVES 2

PREP TIME: 25 MINUTES / FINISH TIME: 5 MINUTES / TOTAL TIME: 30 MINUTES

DAIRY-FREE

This is the dish that really got me into cooking. I made black and white sesame seed–crusted ahi tuna with a mango salsa and served it beachside with peach Bellinis in Santa Barbara where I went to college. It was in that moment I realized I can cook anything as long as I make an honest attempt at it and am not scared to try it. Here's the recipe that started it all!

2 (4- to 5-ounce) ahi tuna steaks **P**
⅓ cup Asian Soy Vinaigrette (page 147)
¾ cup mixed black and white
    sesame seeds **T**
1 large orange, peeled and cubed **V**
1 medium avocado, cubed **B**
¼ cup loosely packed cilantro leaves **V**
Juice of ½ lime
¼ cup grapeseed, vegetable, canola,
    or other neutral oil

1. Gently run the tuna steaks under cold water, then pat them dry with a paper towel. Place the steaks in a large resealable bag and add the vinaigrette. Seal the bag tightly and refrigerate for 15 minutes to marinate.

2. While the tuna marinates, place the sesame seeds on a large plate.

3. Place the orange and avocado cubes in a small bowl. Finely chop the cilantro and add to the orange and avocado. Drizzle with the lime juice and toss to combine. The lime juice prevents the avocado from browning (oxidizing). Set aside.

4. Heat the oil in a large skillet over medium-high heat until it is scorching.

5. While the oil heats, remove the tuna steaks from the marinade. Press the tuna into the sesame seeds to coat evenly on all sides. Place the tuna in the hot oil, and sear the steaks for about 45 seconds on one side, then flip and sear for about 30 seconds on the other side. The tuna will still be very rare in the middle. If you prefer your steaks more well done, increase the cooking time until they reach your desired doneness. Transfer the tuna to a cutting board and slice.

6. Divide the citrus-avocado salsa between two bowls. Top with the sliced tuna. Serve at room temperature.

TECHNIQUE TIP: As raw tuna cooks, it turns from pink to brown. The pinker it is, the rarer it is. When you place the raw tuna into the hot oil, it will turn brown from the bottom to the top. This way, you have control over how rare you cook your tuna.

PER SERVING

Calories: 984; Fat: 79g; Sodium: 1,525mg; Carbohydrates: 37g; Protein: 42g; Fiber: 15g

THAI CHICKEN AND PEANUT SALAD

SERVES 4

PREP TIME: 30 MINUTES / FINISH TIME: 5 MINUTES / TOTAL TIME: 35 MINUTES

GLUTEN-FREE, DAIRY-FREE

Sometimes you need your easy dinner salad to be even easier. Enter the whole-roasted rotisserie chicken. It is an extremely versatile and quick solution for weeknight salads. This salad is nutty, fresh, and satisfying.

1 cup jasmine rice **B**
1 large rotisserie chicken **P**
1 large carrot **V**
¼ cup loosely packed cilantro leaves **B**
½ cup peanuts **T**
½ cup Cilantro-Lime Dressing (page 152)
Juice of 1 lime

1. Combine the rice and 2 cups of water in a large pot and cook according to the instructions on page 14.

2. While the rice cooks, cut the chicken into bite-size pieces, slice the carrot into thin rounds, and finely chop the cilantro leaves.

3. Toast the peanuts in a small skillet according to the instructions on page 15.

4. Divide the rice, chicken, and carrot among four bowls. Top with the chopped cilantro, toasted peanuts, and dressing. Drizzle with the lime juice for added freshness. Serve warm.

FREEZER TIP: To cut down on cooking time, buy pre-frozen rice. It is prepared in a matter of minutes by quick-steaming in the microwave. This is a handy trick, and it's highly recommended to always have a few emergency packages of frozen grains in the freezer.

SUBSTITUTION TIP: Use basmati or another long-grain rice in place of the jasmine rice.

PER SERVING

Calories: 692; Fat: 39g; Sodium: 127mg; Carbohydrates: 47g; Protein: 40g; Fiber: 2g

INDIAN CURRIED LENTIL AND PANEER SALAD

SERVES 4

PREP TIME: 35 MINUTES / FINISH TIME: 5 MINUTES / TOTAL TIME: 40 MINUTES

VEGETARIAN, GLUTEN-FREE, NUT-FREE

You can't talk about Asian food without talking about South Asia: the foods that come from India, Pakistan, Bhutan, Nepal, Sri Lanka, and the Maldives. Curry is a spice that is featured in much of South and East Asian cooking, but it never ceases to amaze me how different those flavors are depending on the region. This Indian-inspired curried lentil and paneer salad is spicy and satisfying.

1 cup green lentils **P**

½ pound paneer, cut into cubes **T**

1 teaspoon curry powder

¼ teaspoon turmeric

2 tablespoons ghee (clarified butter) or neutral oil, like grapeseed or canola

1 large red or yellow bell pepper, thinly sliced **V**

2 large shallots or 1 small onion, thinly sliced **B**

2 large garlic cloves, minced

6 cups baby spinach **B**

½ cup Cumin-Mint Yogurt Dressing (page 162)

1. Rinse the lentils under cold water. Cook them according to the instructions on page 14.

2. While the lentils cook, place the paneer cubes in a small bowl and toss with the curry powder and turmeric.

3. Heat the ghee in a medium skillet over medium-high heat. When hot, add the paneer cubes and sear until golden brown on all sides, about 5 minutes total. Transfer the paneer to a paper towel-lined plate and set aside. Drain any excess fat from the skillet, but do not wipe it out.

4. Add the bell pepper and shallots to the skillet. Cook, stirring occasionally, for about 5 minutes, or until softened. Add the garlic and continue cooking for another 2 minutes. Reduce the heat to low and add the lentils and paneer to the skillet. Stir to combine.

5. Divide the spinach among four plates. Top with the paneer and lentil mixture. Drizzle with the dressing and serve warm.

INGREDIENT TIP: Paneer is a cheese that is made in a similar way as Italian mozzarella. It is creamy and smooth, and can be cut and molded to make any shape. If you can't find paneer, use fresh mozzarella instead.

PER SERVING

Calories: 390; Fat: 16g; Sodium: 420mg; Carbohydrates: 44g; Protein: 18g; Fiber: 17g

FORBIDDEN RICE, MANGO, AVOCADO, AND ALMOND SALAD

SERVES 4

PREP TIME: 30 MINUTES / FINISH TIME: 5 MINUTES / TOTAL TIME: 35 MINUTES

VEGETARIAN, DAIRY-FREE

Don't let the title fool you—this salad is encouraged, not forbidden. Forbidden rice is a nutritious dark-black rice, and it pairs seamlessly with East Asian ingredients. Sweet, tangy, nutty, and chewy, this salad will play with your taste buds.

1 cup forbidden rice B
1 large mango V
1 large avocado B
¼ small red onion B
½ cup slivered almonds T
½ cup Asian Soy Vinaigrette (page 147)

1. Combine the rice and 2 cups of water in a large pot. Cook according to the instructions on page 14.

2. While the rice cooks, dice the mango and avocado, and mince the red onion.

3. In a small skillet, toast the almonds until golden brown according to the instructions on page 15.

4. Divide the rice among four bowls. Add the mango, avocado, and red onion. Drizzle with the vinaigrette and top with the toasted almonds. Serve warm.

TECHNIQUE TIP: To cube a mango, use a large, sharp knife and cut the mango lengthwise on one side, getting as close as possible to the seed. Repeat on the other side of the mango. Fruit-side up, make vertical and horizontal slits into each slice with the knife, then bend the mango back with both hands. This will invert it and expose the cubed mango pieces. Cut the cubes off of the peel at the base of the slits.

SUBSTITUTION TIP: If you have trouble finding forbidden rice, you can use brown or white rice instead.

PER SERVING

Calories: 331; Fat: 22g; Sodium: 1,465mg; Carbohydrates: 35g; Protein: 8g; Fiber: 7g

CURRIED EGG SALAD BOATS

SERVES 4
PREP TIME: 15 MINUTES / FINISH TIME: 5 MINUTES / TOTAL TIME: 20 MINUTES
VEGETARIAN, GLUTEN-FREE, NUT-FREE, DAIRY-FREE

Play with your food! This is a great salad for introducing kids to new flavors. And what's better than playing with your food? Let them construct their own lettuce-leaf boats with this quick, easy, Indian-inspired egg salad.

8 large eggs P
¼ cup mayonnaise
1 teaspoon curry powder
1 tablespoon minced chives B
Salt
Freshly ground black pepper
12 Bibb lettuce leaves B
¼ teaspoon paprika, for garnish (optional)

1. Hard-boil the eggs according to the instructions on page 14.
2. Once cool, peel and dice the eggs, then put them in a large bowl. Add the mayonnaise, curry powder, and chives. Season with salt and pepper. Stir to combine.
3. Place the Bibb lettuce leaves on a cutting board or plate. Spoon some curried egg salad into each leaf. Dust with the paprika (if using) for a subtle bit of additional flavor.

INGREDIENT TIP: Eggs are truly universal and can take on the flavor of any cuisine, which makes them a fantastic complement to Indian spices.

SUBSTITUTION TIP: Use romaine or butter lettuce in place of Bibb lettuce.

PER SERVING

Calories: 403; Fat: 15g; Sodium: 284mg; Carbohydrates: 5g; Protein: 13g; Fiber: 0g

BLOOD ORANGE, MANGO, EDAMAME, AND CHICKEN SALAD

SERVES 4

PREP TIME: 10 MINUTES / FINISH TIME: 5 MINUTES / TOTAL TIME: 15 MINUTES

NUT-FREE, DAIRY-FREE

Fruity, acidic, colorful, and rich, this quick salad is loaded with bright and healthy flavors. Many people aren't familiar with blood oranges, so this fruit can provide a shock of delight when encountered for the first time—first with their unexpected and vibrant red color, then with their flavor. I love seeing the look of wonder on someone's face when they try something new and unexpected. It's all part of my (not at all) diabolical plan.

6 cups mizuna greens (Japanese mustard greens) B
2 blood oranges, peeled and cut into wedges V
1 mango, cubed V
1 cup shelled edamame B
1 rotisserie chicken, cut into bite-size pieces P
½ cup Asian Soy Vinaigrette (page 147)

1. In a large bowl, combine the mizuna greens, orange wedges, mango cubes, edamame, and chicken. Drizzle with the vinaigrette and toss to combine.

2. Divide among four plates and serve at room temperature.

INGREDIENT TIP: Blood oranges are truly a work of nature's art. They are distinctly bright red on the inside and have a subtle raspberry-like flavor, making them sweeter and less acidic than other citrus fruits.

SUBSTITUTION TIP: Use baby spring mix in place of mizuna greens and regular oranges in place of blood oranges.

PER SERVING

Calories: 426; Fat: 16g; Sodium: 1,681mg; Carbohydrates: 32g; Protein: 39g; Fiber: 9g

SHAVED BRUSSELS SPROUT AND SHRIMP SALAD

SERVES 4

PREP TIME: 10 MINUTES / FINISH TIME: 5 MINUTES / TOTAL TIME: 15 MINUTES

DAIRY-FREE

Raw shaved Brussels sprouts are crunchy like cabbage and have a similar taste. Most people only think of them roasted (definitely delicious!), but raw and prepared like slaw, they are a revelation. Paired with shrimp and bold Asian flavors like soy and ginger, this dish makes for an extremely fast and easy dinner salad.

4 cups Brussels sprouts, thinly sliced **B**
2 large carrots, thinly sliced **V**
¼ cup loosely packed cilantro leaves, finely chopped **B**
½ cup Asian Soy Vinaigrette (page 147)
½ cup peanuts **T**
1 tablespoon sesame oil
1 pound shrimp, peeled and deveined **P**

1. Place the Brussels sprouts, carrots, and cilantro in a large bowl. Add the vinaigrette and toss to combine. Set aside.

2. Toast the peanuts in a small skillet according to the instructions on page 15.

3. Heat the oil in a large skillet over medium-high heat. Once hot, add the shrimp and cook until pink on all sides, 2 to 3 minutes per side. Transfer the shrimp to the bowl with the Brussels sprout mixture. Toss to combine.

4. Divide the salad among four plates and top with the toasted peanuts. Serve at room temperature.

FREEZER TIP: Always keep a package of frozen shrimp in your freezer. They thaw quickly and make for the fastest, easiest addition of delicious protein to any salad.

PER SERVING

Calories: 345; Fat: 19g; Sodium: 1,642mg; Carbohydrates: 19g; Protein: 32g; Fiber: 6g

ASIAN PASTA SALAD

SERVES 4

PREP TIME: 20 MINUTES / FINISH TIME: 5 MINUTES / TOTAL TIME: 25 MINUTES

NUT-FREE, DAIRY-FREE

Pasta salad isn't just for Italian preparations. Pasta itself is such a neutral flavor that it soaks in the flavors of whatever is added to it. That makes it worthy of using to create salads with flavors from around the world, including this Asian-inspired one. It will make you rethink what a pasta salad can be.

1½ cups rotini pasta B
1 tablespoon sesame oil
2 garlic cloves, minced
1 cup sugar snap peas V
2 cups broccoli florets V
3 large scallions, green parts only, thinly sliced T
1 large rotisserie chicken, cut into bite-size pieces P
½ cup Asian Soy Vinaigrette (page 147)

1. Bring a large pot of salted water to a boil. Add a drop or two of oil to the water to prevent the pasta from sticking together. Add the rotini and cook until al dente, about 8 minutes (or follow the package instructions). Drain.

2. Heat the sesame oil in a large skillet over medium-high heat. When hot, add the garlic and cook until aromatic, about 1 minute. Add the sugar snap peas, broccoli, and scallions. Cook for about 5 minutes, stirring occasionally.

3. Add the pasta to the vegetables and stir to combine. Mix in the chicken. Turn off the heat and add the vinaigrette. Toss to combine.

4. Divide the salad among four bowls. It can be served warm or cold.

MAKE-AHEAD TIP: This recipe can easily be doubled, tripled, or quadrupled and made in bulk in advance. The longer it sits, the deeper the flavors become. So you can have your dinner, then lunch the next day.

PER SERVING

Calories: 476; Fat: 18g; Sodium: 1,574mg; Carbohydrates: 42g; Protein: 41g; Fiber: 4g

ASPARAGUS, PROSCIUTTO, AND POACHED EGG SALAD *page 52*

CHAPTER 4

EUROPEAN-INSPIRED SALADS

When I think of European food, I think of French cheese, Belgian waffles, Russian potato salad, and Scandinavian smoked salmon, to name a few. I've taken these ingredients and turned them into the salads of your European dreams. Wishing you were living *la vie en rose* in Paris? Try the Croissant Croque Monsieur Salad (page 58). Or missing Munich's Oktoberfest? Try the German Schnitzel Caesar Salad (page 56). I've taken the heartiness of traditional European meat-and-potato-heavy dishes as well as the fresh fruits, vegetables, and cheeses that Europeans have elevated to a fine art as inspiration for these salads. Dinner is served.

ASPARAGUS, PROSCIUTTO, AND POACHED EGG SALAD

SERVES 4

PREP TIME: 20 MINUTES / FINISH TIME: 5 MINUTES / TOTAL TIME 25 MINUTES

GLUTEN-FREE, NUT-FREE, DAIRY-FREE

APE is the new BLT. Just like bacon, lettuce, and tomato (hey, they make for a great salad, too!), asparagus, prosciutto, and egg are a classic combination. The crisp earthiness of asparagus with the saltiness of prosciutto and the velvety, rich texture of an egg have launched many a brunch. I've just turned the combo on its head and made it into a delicious dinner salad.

1 bunch fresh asparagus, trimmed **V**
2 tablespoons extra-virgin olive oil
Salt
Freshly ground black pepper
8 eggs, poached **T**
12 slices prosciutto **P**
6 cups baby arugula **B**
½ cup Lemon Vinaigrette (page 146)

1. Preheat the oven to 350°F.
2. Cut the asparagus on the diagonal into 2- to 3-inch pieces. Place them on a baking sheet. Drizzle with the olive oil and season with salt and pepper. Toss to combine. Roast for about 15 minutes, or until the pieces are crisp-tender when pierced with a fork.
3. While the asparagus roasts, poach the eggs according to the instructions on page 14.
4. Slice the prosciutto into ribbons and place in a large bowl along with the arugula. Drizzle with the vinaigrette and toss to combine.

5. Add the roasted asparagus to the bowl and toss to combine.
6. Divide the salad among four plates. Top each with 2 poached eggs. Serve while the eggs are still warm.

OPTIONAL TIP: Add some grilled chicken for a protein-packed post-workout dinner.

SUBSTITUTION TIP: The prosciutto can be substituted with salami or other cured pork.

PER SERVING

Calories: 572; Fat: 50g; Sodium: 1,541mg; Carbohydrates: 4g; Protein: 32g; Fiber: 2g

ROASTED GARLIC, BEET, AND GOAT CHEESE SALAD

SERVES 3

PREP TIME: 1 HOUR 5 MINUTES / FINISH TIME: 5 MINUTES / TOTAL TIME: 1 HOUR 10 MINUTES

VEGETARIAN, GLUTEN-FREE

Nothing *beets* perfectly roasted beets with garlic and goat cheese. What can I say? I love a good pun. I also love this salad. Beets are amazingly earthy in flavor. They're also a great source of potassium and vitamin C.

3 medium beets B
2 tablespoons extra-virgin olive oil
1 head garlic
6 tablespoons Lemon Vinaigrette (page 146)
1 cup fresh parsley, roughly chopped V
Salt
Freshly ground black pepper
1 pound crumbled goat cheese P
1 cup sunflower seeds T

1. Preheat the oven to 400°F.

2. Cut off the root ends of the beets and scrub them clean. Rub them all over with the olive oil. Wrap each one loosely in aluminum foil.

3. Cut the non-root end off the head of garlic and wrap it loosely in aluminum foil. Place it and the beets on a baking sheet. Roast for about 25 minutes, then remove the garlic. Continue roasting the beets for about 20 minutes (about 45 minutes in total), or until a knife cuts through them smoothly.

4. Let the garlic cool for 5 minutes, or until it can be handled with your hands. Squeeze the garlic head from the root end up toward the cut end. The garlic cloves should be soft and should pop out easily. Roughly chop the cloves and put them in a large bowl.

5. Let the beets cool for about 10 minutes before handling. Holding them in a paper towel, peel the skins off. Dice the peeled beets and put them in the bowl with the garlic.

6. Drizzle the beets with the vinaigrette and toss to combine. Add the parsley and toss to combine.

7. Season the salad with the salt and pepper. Divide among three bowls and top with the goat cheese. Garnish with the sunflower seeds.

INGREDIENT TIP: Be careful with red beets, because they stain quickly and easily! Be sure to peel them in the sink and, ideally, wear gloves, because they will temporarily stain your skin.

MAKE-AHEAD TIP: This salad tastes better if the beets marinate in the vinaigrette for at least 24 hours. The flavors really seep into the beets and intensify. Add the parsley, goat cheese, and sunflower seeds right before serving.

PER SERVING

Calories: 882; Fat: 69g; Sodium: 722mg; Carbohydrates: 18g; Protein: 22g; Fiber: 4g

MOTHER RUSSIA TUNA SALAD

SERVES 2

PREP TIME: 20 MINUTES / FINISH TIME: 5 MINUTES / TOTAL TIME: 25 MINUTES

GLUTEN-FREE, NUT-FREE, DAIRY-FREE

When I was little, I always helped my mom in the kitchen. I started as a dishwasher, turned into the table setter, and then graduated to salad maker, then to sous chef, and finally to head chef. This was one of the first salads I ever learned to make under my mom's tutelage, and I've been making it ever since.

5 eggs B

2 (6-ounce) cans chunk light tuna packed in water P

5 large Mediterranean pickles or your preferred pickle V

3 tablespoons mayonnaise

¼ teaspoon salt

¼ teaspoon ground cumin

½ cup drained canned sweet corn (optional)

6 Bibb lettuce leaves B

1. Hard-boil the eggs according to the instructions on page 14. Once cool, peel and dice them, then place in a medium bowl.

2. Drain the tuna and add to the bowl. Use a fork to flake the fish.

3. Dice the pickles and add them to the bowl.

4. Add the mayonnaise, salt, and cumin and mix until well combined. Stir in the corn (if using).

5. Place 3 lettuce leaves on each of two plates. Divide the tuna salad among the lettuce leaves. Serve cold.

OPTIONAL TIP: Corn adds extra sweetness, body, and fiber to the salad. It's a trick I learned from my aunt. It might sound strange, but try it out for a pleasant and unexpected twist.

PER SERVING

Calories: 411; Fat: 20g; Sodium: 3,726mg; Carbohydrates: 21g; Protein: 38g; Fiber: 5g

SMOKED SALMON AND EGG SALAD

SERVES 4

PREP TIME: 15 MINUTES / FINISH TIME: 5 MINUTES / TOTAL TIME: 20 MINUTES

GLUTEN-FREE, NUT-FREE, DAIRY-FREE

Smoked salmon and eggs are perfect for brunch—but also perfect for salads. They pack a ton of protein and healthy fats. Smoked salmon is definitely a treat, though less so to your wallet. But when you want to splurge or it's a special occasion, it's definitely worth the bit of extra expense.

8 eggs T
8 cups mixed greens B
½ cup Lemon Vinaigrette (page 146)
2 large Persian cucumbers, halved lengthwise and cut into half-moons V
1½ tablespoons pickled red onions (page 13) B
8 ounces smoked salmon lox P
Salt
Freshly ground black pepper

1. Soft-boil the eggs according to the instructions on page 14. Peel and set aside.

2. In a large bowl, toss the mixed greens with the vinaigrette. Add the cucumbers and pickled red onions and toss to combine.

3. Divide the salad among four plates. Gently pull apart the lox slices and add some to each salad. Halve the soft-boiled eggs lengthwise and top each salad with them. Season generously with salt and pepper. Serve while the eggs are warm.

MAKE-AHEAD TIP: I always keep a jar of pickled red onions on hand. They pack tremendous flavor. In this salad in particular, they help cut through the fattiness of the smoked salmon and the eggs while complementing them at the same time. Follow the instructions on page 13 to make them.

PER SERVING

Calories: 603; Fat: 44g; Sodium: 386mg; Carbohydrates: 12g; Protein: 44g; Fiber: 1g

GERMAN SCHNITZEL CAESAR SALAD

SERVES 4

PREP TIME: 20 MINUTES / FINISH TIME: 5 MINUTES / TOTAL TIME: 25 MINUTES

NUT-FREE

Schnitzel: the quintessential, must-eat German dish. What can possibly go wrong when chicken, pork, or veal cutlets are tenderized, breaded, and pan-fried? It's a basic preparation that everyone will love. Throw a schnitzel into a salad to pack a punch of tender protein and create a salad everyone will look forward to.

2 large chicken breasts
　(about 1⅓ pounds total) P
2 cups Italian bread crumbs
1 large egg, beaten
¾ cup all-purpose flour
Salt
Freshly ground black pepper
Grapeseed, canola, or vegetable oil,
　for frying
½ lemon
6 cups shredded romaine lettuce B
¼ cup Lemon Vinaigrette (page 146)
1½ cups croutons T
2 cups cherry tomatoes, halved V
½ cup shredded Parmesan cheese B

1. Butterfly the chicken breasts according to the instructions on page 33.

2. Add the bread crumbs to a large plate. Place the beaten egg in a shallow bowl. Add the flour to another large plate and season it with the salt and pepper. Line up the flour, beaten egg, and bread crumbs in a row.

3. Dredge each piece of chicken in the flour to coat completely, then dip it in the egg. Place the chicken on the bread crumbs and firmly press down to coat on one side. Turn over and press down to coat on the other side. Transfer to a plate.

4. Heat the oil in a large skillet over medium-high heat. Once hot, add one piece of chicken and pan-fry until golden brown on both sides, about 5 minutes per side. Transfer to a paper towel-lined plate and repeat with the second piece of chicken. To speed up the cooking process, use two skillets to fry the chicken.

5. Squeeze fresh lemon juice over the chicken, then slice the chicken into cubes.

6. Place the lettuce in a large bowl and drizzle with the vinaigrette. Toss to combine.

7. Divide the salad, croutons, tomatoes, and chicken among four plates. Top with the Parmesan. Serve while the chicken is warm.

OPTIONAL TIP: You can substitute pork or veal cutlets for the chicken. You can also make lettuce wraps out of this recipe. Skip the shredded romaine and scoop the chicken, tomatoes, croutons, and Parmesan into Bibb, romaine, or butter lettuce cups. Drizzle with some of the vinaigrette and enjoy.

PER SERVING

Calories: 955; Fat: 40g; Sodium: 1,134mg; Carbohydrates: 87g; Protein: 65g; Fiber: 7g

RUSSIAN POTATO SALAD
(SALAT OLIVIER)

SERVES 2

PREP TIME: 25 MINUTES / FINISH TIME: 5 MINUTES / TOTAL TIME: 30 MINUTES

VEGETARIAN, GLUTEN-FREE, NUT-FREE, DAIRY-FREE

You can't attend a Russian gathering without seeing this potato salad on the table. It includes carrots, eggs, sweet peas, and pickles, and is as old-school Russian as pumpkin pie is American. No one will raise an eyebrow if you serve it with some ice-cold vodka. To your health!

2 large potatoes, peeled B
4 large carrots, peeled V
4 eggs P
1 (15-ounce) can sweet green peas, drained B
4 large Mediterranean pickles or your preferred pickle, diced T
Salt
Freshly ground black pepper
Pinch paprika
¼ cup mayonnaise

1. Bring a large pot of salted water to a boil. Add the potatoes and carrots and boil for about 15 minutes, or until tender when pierced with a fork. (Alternatively, cut the potatoes and carrots into smaller pieces for a faster cooking time.) Once cooked through, drain the potatoes and carrots and rinse thoroughly with cold water to stop the cooking process.

2. While the potatoes and carrots are cooking, hard-boil the eggs according to the instructions on page 14. Peel, dice, and place them in a large bowl.

3. Add the peas and pickles to the bowl.

4. Cut the potatoes and carrots into bite-size pieces and add to the bowl. Season with salt, pepper, and the paprika. Add the mayonnaise and mix until well combined. Serve cold.

OPTIONAL TIP: Traditionally, bologna slices are diced and added to this salad. They add a nice meaty, salty undertone that works well with the rest of the ingredients. You can also add beets, grilled chicken, olives, green onions, and/ or mustard. The possibilities are endless.

PER SERVING

Calories: 517; Fat: 19g; Sodium: 4,058mg; Carbohydrates: 70g; Protein: 20g; Fiber: 14g

CROISSANT CROQUE MONSIEUR SALAD

SERVES 3 OR 4

PREP TIME: 5 MINUTES / FINISH TIME: 5 MINUTES / TOTAL TIME: 10 MINUTES

NUT-FREE

This salad takes a classic croque monsieur—a French ham and Swiss cheese sandwich—to the next level by using a croissant, and then transforming it all into a quick salad you can whip up in 10 minutes. Ooh la la!

2 large croissants **B**
Salt
Freshly ground black pepper
6 cups mesclun mix or mixed baby greens **B**
½ cup Honey-Mustard Vinaigrette (page 150)
8 ounces cured ham, cubed **P**
6 ounces Swiss cheese, cubed **T**
2 cups cherry tomatoes, halved **V**

1. Cut croissants into bite-size cubes. In a large skillet over medium-high heat, toast the cubes until they turn into crispy croutons, no more than 5 minutes. No oil or butter is necessary since the croissants have a high butter content. Transfer the toasted cubes to a plate and lightly season them with salt and pepper. Set aside.

2. Place the mesclun mix in a large bowl and drizzle with the vinaigrette. Toss to combine.

3. To the bowl, add the ham, Swiss cheese, and cherry tomatoes and toss to combine.

4. Divide the salad among three or four plates and top with the croissant croutons.

LEFTOVER TIP: This is a fun, creative way to utilize leftover croissants and really elevate them in a salad for dinner the next night.

OPTIONAL TIP: Turn the croque monsieur salad into a croque madame salad by adding a poached egg on top.

PER SERVING
Calories: 828; Fat: 55g; Sodium: 2,473mg; Carbohydrates: 36g; Protein: 48g; Fiber: 5g

BELGIAN WAFFLE FRUIT SALAD

SERVES 2

PREP TIME: 15 MINUTES / FINISH TIME: 5 MINUTES / TOTAL TIME: 20 MINUTES

VEGETARIAN, NUT-FREE

Sometimes you just want to skip dinner and go straight to dessert. Fruit salad with Belgian waffle "croutons" will satisfy your sweet tooth while still giving you some always-welcome vitamins and nutrition at the end of the day. Or, if you prefer, think of it as breakfast for dinner.

2 cups sliced strawberries **V**
1 cup blueberries or raspberries **V**
1 orange, peeled and cut into wedges **V**
1 tablespoon sugar
2 large store-bought Belgian waffles **B**
2 tablespoons unsalted butter
¼ cup loosely packed fresh mint leaves, cut into thin strips **T**

1. Place the strawberries, blueberries, and orange wedges in a large bowl. Sprinkle with the sugar to macerate the fruit (see Technique tip). Let sit for at least 15 minutes.

2. Toast the Belgian waffles in your toaster according to the package instructions. Once toasted, cut the waffles into cubes.

3. In a large skillet over high heat, melt the butter. Add the cubed waffles. Cook until toasted on all sides, about 5 minutes. Remove the skillet from the heat.

4. Divide the fruit among two bowls and top with the waffle croutons and fresh mint. Serve at room temperature.

TECHNIQUE TIP: Macerating fruit is an easy, powerful culinary trick anyone can do. It makes the fruit much more flavorful. Simply stir a bit of sugar into a bowl of fruit and let sit for at least 15 minutes. The fruit will release its natural juices while it rests. This is a great hack, especially if your fruit isn't fully ripe.

OPTIONAL TIP: Add some walnuts or almonds for an added crunch and protein content.

PER SERVING
Calories: 432; Fat: 16g; Sodium: 283mg; Carbohydrates: 69g; Protein: 8g; Fiber: 10g

ASHKENAZI APPLE, WALNUT, AND DATE SALAD (CHAROSET)

SERVES 4

PREP TIME: 15 MINUTES / FINISH TIME: 5 MINUTES / TOTAL TIME: 20 MINUTES

VEGETARIAN, GLUTEN-FREE, DAIRY-FREE

Typically eaten as part of the Passover celebration, this Ashkenazi (European Jewish) salad can be eaten year-round and is absolutely delicious. Who says fruit salads can't be well balanced? Pairing fresh fruit with dried fruit can be a revelation. The different textures are unexpected and the concentrated sweetness of the dried fruit is offset by the subtler sweetness of fresh fruit.

1 cup walnuts or almonds **T**

3 large apples, ideally Gala, Honeycrisp, or Fuji, peeled, cored, and diced **B**

½ cup dried dates, pitted and cubed **V**

½ cup dried apricots or cranberries **V**

Grated zest and juice of ½ lemon

¼ teaspoon ground cinnamon

1 tablespoon honey

1. Lightly toast the walnuts according to the instructions on page 15.

2. Place the apples, dates, and apricots in a large bowl. Add the lemon zest and juice, the toasted nuts, cinnamon, and honey. Stir to combine.

3. Divide the fruit salad among four bowls. Serve cold or at room temperature.

MAKE-AHEAD TIP: For ideal results, refrigerate the salad for at least 8 hours. This resting time builds deeper flavors and lets the natural sugars of the apples really develop from the added honey.

PER SERVING

Calories: 752; Fat: 34g; Sodium: 8mg; Carbohydrates: 117g; Protein: 10g; Fiber: 18g

FRENCH BRIE FRUIT SALAD

PREP TIME: 15 MINUTES / FINISH TIME: 5 MINUTES / TOTAL TIME: 20 MINUTES

VEGETARIAN, GLUTEN-FREE

Sweet, juicy fruit, crunchy toasted nuts, and creamy, rich Brie cheese—what is often found on a cheese board is now turned into a tempting salad. This perfect combo is just the ticket on an early autumn night when apples and pears have come into season. Sign me up.

1 cup walnuts or almonds T
2 large apples, preferably Gala, Honeycrisp, or Fuji, peeled, cored, and diced B
2 large pears, diced V
2 cups green or purple grapes, halved B
¼ teaspoon ground cinnamon
1 tablespoon honey
6 ounces Brie cheese P

1. Lightly toast the walnuts according to the instructions on page 15.

2. Combine the apples, pears, grapes, toasted nuts, cinnamon, and honey in a large bowl.

3. Cut the Brie into thin, bite-size pieces.

4. Divide the fruit salad between two or three bowls. Top with the Brie. Serve cold or at room temperature.

OPTIONAL TIP: For a sharper flavor, replace the Brie with a stronger cheese such as Roquefort, Gorgonzola, or feta. The salty contrast to the sweet and nutty ingredients works deliciously.

PER SERVING
Calories: 942; Fat: 57g; Sodium: 542mg; Carbohydrates: 95g; Protein: 27g; Fiber: 16g

STEAK, PEAR, AND ROQUEFORT SALAD

SERVES 2

PREP TIME: 40 MINUTES / FINISH TIME: 5 MINUTES / TOTAL TIME: 45 MINUTES

GLUTEN-FREE, NUT-FREE

Sweet, savory, spicy, sharp, and sultry, this steak salad is filling and hits all the flavor notes you could want for dinner. Steak with a blue cheese like Roquefort is a classic you'll see on the menu at steak houses. Lucky for me, the combination makes for a great salad, too.

2 tablespoons extra-virgin olive oil
1 garlic clove, minced
1 rosemary sprig or 1 teaspoon
    dried rosemary
2 (4-ounce) flank steaks **P**
1 large pear **V**
Salt
Freshly ground black pepper
1 tablespoon unsalted butter
4 cups baby arugula **B**
¼ cup Buttermilk-Poppy Dressing
    (page 153)
¼ cup crumbled Roquefort cheese **T**

1. Preheat the oven to 375°F.

2. In a resealable bag, combine the olive oil, garlic, rosemary, and flank steaks. Seal the bag and massage the meat to coat it in the marinade. Set aside to marinate for about 15 minutes.

3. Slice the pear and set aside.

4. Remove the steaks from the marinade (discarding the liquid) and season generously on both sides with salt and pepper. Heat a large oven-safe skillet over high heat. Once hot, add the steaks and sear on both sides, about 2 minutes per side. Transfer the skillet to the oven and continue cooking for 10 minutes.

5. Remove the skillet from the oven and place back on the stove over medium-high heat. Add the butter to melt. Using a spoon, baste the steaks with the melted butter for 2 minutes. Remove the skillet from the heat, cover with aluminum foil, and let the steaks rest for 5 minutes before slicing against the grain into strips.

6. Place the arugula in a large bowl and drizzle with the dressing. Toss to combine.

7. Divide the arugula, steak, and pear between two plates. Top with the Roquefort. Serve warm.

SUBSTITUTION TIP: Just about any type of blue cheese is delicious on this salad. Try Maytag blue, Stilton, or Gorgonzola.

PER SERVING

Calories: 677; Fat: 25g; Sodium: 1,111mg; Carbohydrates: 21g; Protein: 40g; Fiber: 5g

RUSSIAN VINAIGRETTE SALAD

SERVES 2
PREP TIME: 55 MINUTES / FINISH TIME: 5 MINUTES / TOTAL TIME: 1 HOUR
VEGETARIAN, GLUTEN-FREE, NUT-FREE

One of the most classic Russian salads found at almost all Russian gatherings is this "vinaigrette" salad. Roasted beets, potatoes, and carrots are dressed simply in a creamy, garlicky dill and sour cream dressing. The combination makes for a yummy, satisfying, and hearty salad.

1 large beet V
2 teaspoons extra-virgin olive oil
Salt
3 medium Yukon Gold
    potatoes, peeled B
1 large carrot, peeled V
2 or 3 large dill pickles B
¼ cup loosely packed fresh parsley
    leaves, finely chopped T
¼ cup Dill, Lemon, and Garlic Sour
    Cream Dressing (page 159)

1. Preheat the oven to 400°F.

2. Cut the stem off the beet and scrub clean. Rub the beet all over with the olive oil. Wrap loosely in aluminum foil and place on a baking sheet. Roast for about 45 minutes, or until a knife cuts through it smoothly.

3. While the beet roasts, place a large pot of lightly salted water over high heat. Bring to a boil, add the potatoes and carrot, and cook for about 20 minutes. Use a knife to check if the potatoes and carrot are tender. The carrot will be done first.

4. Let the beet cool for about 10 minutes before handling. Holding it in a paper towel, peel off the skin. Dice the beet and place it in a large bowl.

5. Dice the potatoes, carrot, and pickles and add to the beet along with the parsley. Drizzle with the dressing and toss to combine.

6. Divide the salad between two plates. Serve warm or at room temperature.

SHORTCUT TIP: Using canned beets will significantly cut down your cooking time. Quartering or halving the potatoes will also reduce the cooking time.

PER SERVING
Calories: 250; Fat: 10g; Sodium: 2,658mg; Carbohydrates: 39g; Protein: 5g; Fiber: 9g

BLACKBERRY, HAM, AND FIG SALAD

SERVES 2

PREP TIME: 55 MINUTES / FINISH TIME: 5 MINUTES / TOTAL TIME: 1 HOUR

GLUTEN-FREE, NUT-FREE

Sweet, tart, salty, fatty flavors and chewy textures combine for the ultimate quick dinner salad.

2 cups blackberries, halved V
1½ teaspoons sugar, divided
4 or 5 large fresh figs T
2 tablespoons unsalted butter
4 cups frisée B
¼ cup Lemon Vinaigrette (page 146)
8 ounces chunk deli ham, diced P

1. Place the blackberries in a medium bowl. Sprinkle with ½ teaspoon of sugar and set aside to macerate.

2. Slice the figs lengthwise into ⅛-inch-thick slices.

3. In a large skillet over medium-high heat, melt the butter. Add the figs and the remaining 1 teaspoon of sugar and stir to combine. Let the figs caramelize on each side, 6 to 8 minutes total. Remove the skillet from the heat.

4. While the figs caramelize, toss the frisée with the vinaigrette in a large bowl. Add the ham and toss to combine.

5. Divide the salad between two plates. Top with the blackberries, and figs. Serve warm or at room temperature.

TECHNIQUE TIP: Adding sugar to fruit when cooking it helps the caramelization process. It brings an even deeper, warmer feeling to the dish. Fruit naturally caramelizes due to its natural sugar content, but a little bit of added sweetness brings out the flavors even more. Brown sugar that also has molasses in it works well, too, and helps fully develop the flavors.

SUBSTITUTION TIP: Use other berries in place of the blackberries. When in doubt, go with what's in season.

PER SERVING
Calories: 605; Fat: 41g; Sodium: 1,368mg; Carbohydrates: 38g; Protein: 22g; Fiber: 12g

RADISH, CUCUMBER, LOX, AND DILL SALAD

SERVES 2

PREP TIME: 10 MINUTES / FINISH TIME: 5 MINUTES / TOTAL TIME: 15 MINUTES

GLUTEN-FREE, NUT-FREE

This Russian-inspired salad brings together radishes, cucumbers, lox, and dill. They are a classic flavor combination guaranteed to be a hit. Add in toasted pumpernickel or Russian rye bread—why not makes some croutons?—and you'll feel like a true comrade.

2 large radishes, halved and thinly sliced V

4 large Persian cucumbers, halved lengthwise and thinly sliced into half-moons B

¼ cup loosely packed fresh dill, minced T

1 large garlic clove, minced

6 ounces smoked salmon lox P

¼ cup Dill, Lemon, and Garlic Sour Cream Dressing (page 159)

1. Place the radishes, cucumbers, dill, and garlic in a large bowl.

2. Tear the lox into bite-size pieces and add to the bowl. Drizzle with the dressing and toss to combine.

3. Divide the salad between two plates. Serve cold.

INGREDIENT TIP: As a kid, I was always a huge fan of sour cream. I was also a huge fan of sour cream being used in so many Russian dishes. My mom would make these weird-sounding sandwiches that are actually amazing—dark Russian rye bread, sour cream, and sea salt. As odd as that sounds, it's so tangy, creamy, salty, and chewy. This salad is an elevated dedication to the simplest sandwich of my youth.

PER SERVING

Calories: 245; Fat: 9g; Sodium: 1,745mg; Carbohydrates: 25g; Protein: 21g; Fiber: 3g

HONEY-MUSTARD SALMON POTATO SALAD

SERVES 2

PREP TIME: 30 MINUTES / FINISH TIME: 5 MINUTES / TOTAL TIME: 35 MINUTES

GLUTEN-FREE, NUT-FREE

Who needs steak and potatoes when there's salmon and potatoes? And salmon with dill is a classic pairing if there ever was one. The potatoes lend a heartiness that absorbs the gentle flavors of the other ingredients. This potato salad loaded with flavor makes its way to your dinner table via Scandinavia—Sweden, to be specific.

½ cup honey mustard, divided
¾ cup loosely packed fresh dill, minced and divided **T**
1 garlic clove, crushed
2 (5-ounce) salmon fillets **P**
2 large Yukon Gold potatoes **B**
Salt
1 tablespoon extra-virgin olive oil
Freshly ground black pepper
2 tablespoons unsalted butter
1 large garlic clove, minced
Juice of 1 lemon

1. In a small bowl, combine ¼ cup of honey mustard with ¼ cup of dill and the crushed garlic. Rub the salmon fillets all over with this marinade. Set aside to marinate for about 15 minutes.

2. Fill a large pot with water and add the potatoes and a pinch of salt. Bring the water to a boil and cook the potatoes until a knife runs through them easily, 20 to 25 minutes. Drain. Let the potatoes cool for a few minutes, then cut into thick, bite-size pieces.

3. Heat the oil in a skillet over medium-high heat. Season the salmon generously on both sides with salt and pepper. Once the oil is hot, cook the salmon according to the instructions on page 15. Transfer to a large bowl and flake with a fork.

4. Add the potatoes, butter, minced garlic, the remaining ½ cup of dill, the remaining ¼ cup of honey mustard, and the lemon juice. Toss to combine. Season to taste with salt and pepper.

5. Divide the salad between two plates. Serve warm.

TECHNIQUE TIP: To cut the cooking time of the potatoes, halve or quarter them first.

PER SERVING
Calories: 463; Fat: 22g; Sodium: 516mg; Carbohydrates: 38g; Protein: 22g; Fiber: 2g

TUNA NIÇOISE SALAD

SERVES 3 OR 4

PREP TIME: 15 MINUTES / FINISH TIME: 5 MINUTES / TOTAL TIME: 20 MINUTES

GLUTEN-FREE, NUT-FREE, DAIRY-FREE

Time to chop up the ingredients for this classic French salad. A traditional niçoise salad presents the components separately on the plate rather than tossed together. Certainly, you can do that if you like. But since everything is eventually mixed together on the plate, I'm just as happy to skip the intricate presentation.

6 eggs B
6 cups romaine lettuce, torn into bite-size pieces B
2 (6-ounce) cans tuna in water, drained P
¾ cup black or green olives, or your preferred olives, pitted and halved T
1 cup cherry tomatoes, halved V
6 tablespoons Honey-Mustard Vinaigrette (page 150)

1. Hard-boil the eggs according to the instructions on page 14. Peel, then cut them crosswise into thick slices.

2. In a large bowl, add the romaine, tuna, olives, and tomatoes. Drizzle with the vinaigrette and toss to combine.

3. Divide the salad among three or four plates. Top with the egg slices. Serve at room temperature.

OPTIONAL TIP: Similar to a Cobb salad, this salad is a combination of different chopped ingredients, so you have a ton of flexibility to make it your own. Substitute ahi tuna or salmon for the canned tuna, or use green beans, beans, and or/pickles. In other words, mix it up!

PER SERVING
Calories: 562; Fat: 39g; Sodium: 1,881mg; Carbohydrates: 18g; Protein: 39g; Fiber: 7g

RUSSIAN LAYERED HERRING SALAD (SHUBA)

SERVES 2

PREP TIME: 1 HOUR / FINISH TIME: 5 MINUTES / TOTAL TIME: 1 HOUR 5 MINUTES

GLUTEN-FREE, NUT-FREE, DAIRY-FREE

This is a lesson in Russian Salad 101: Take otherwise healthy salads and smother them in mayonnaise. If you want to really go all out, make your own mayonnaise. It only requires egg yolks, lemon juice, vinegar, mustard, and oil. A couple of pulses in the food processor, and what you've created far surpasses what's on the supermarket shelves.

2 large beets, peeled **V**
4 large Yukon Gold potatoes, peeled **B**
4 large carrots, peeled **V**
6 eggs **B**
Salt
Freshly ground black pepper
1 (10-ounce) can smoked herring in oil **P**
⅔ cup mayonnaise

1. Bring a large pot of salted water to a boil. Add the beets, potatoes, and carrots and cook until a knife cuts through them easily, about 20 minutes for the carrots and potatoes and 30 minutes for the beets. Remove the carrots and potatoes when done and continue cooking the beets. When cool enough to handle, dice the potatoes and carrots. Shred the beets using a box grater.

2. Hard-boil the eggs according to the instructions on page 14. Peel and dice them.

3. Build the salad on a large serving plate or platter by constructing layers of the ingredients. Begin with the potatoes and season with salt and pepper, then layer the carrots over them. Add the beets and season with salt and pepper, then layer with the smoked herring. Top with the eggs. Finally, smother the layered salad all over with the mayonnaise, using a spatula to cover the top and sides of the salad. Serve cold.

INGREDIENT TIP: *Shuba* translates to "fur coat" in Russian. This salad is comprised of layers that stack up to look like a coat, and they are then smothered in mayonnaise. This is the ultimate Russian symbol on the table—it's bright pink and absolutely delicious.

SUBSTITUTION TIP: Use canned sardines in place of the herring.

PER SERVING

Calories: 782; Fat: 46g; Sodium: 1,184mg; Carbohydrates: 79g; Protein: 29g; Fiber: 12g

RASPBERRY, ORANGE, GOAT CHEESE, AND CANDIED WALNUT SALAD

SERVES 2

PREP TIME: 10 MINUTES / FINISH TIME: 5 MINUTES / TOTAL TIME: 15 MINUTES

VEGETARIAN, GLUTEN-FREE

Tangy, tart fresh fruit with warm candied, spiced walnuts on a bed of salad greens makes for a satisfying, fruity, and light dinner salad. A basic vinaigrette is all that's needed to complement the flavors of the salad. The lemony dressing enhances the flavors of the fruit and cheese.

2 tablespoons unsalted butter
⅔ cup walnuts 🔲
1 tablespoon sugar
Pinch cayenne pepper (optional)
5 cups spring mix greens 🔲
½ cup fresh raspberries, halved 🔲
1 orange, peeled and cut into wedges 🔲
¼ cup Lemon Vinaigrette (page 146)
½ cup crumbled goat cheese 🔲

1. In a small skillet over medium-high heat, melt the butter. Add the walnuts and toss to evenly coat with the butter. Sprinkle the sugar and cayenne pepper (if using) over the nuts. Let the walnuts caramelize in the sugar, stirring occasionally, about 5 minutes.

2. While the walnuts caramelize, combine the mixed greens, raspberries, and orange wedges in a large bowl. Drizzle with the vinaigrette and toss to combine.

3. Divide the salad between two bowls. Top with the walnuts and goat cheese.

MAKE-AHEAD TIP: Sundays are for candying nuts! Candy walnuts, spice pecans, toast almonds, and prepare many other nut variations. These are so fun to make, and they fill your home with an amazing warm aroma. Plus, you have them on hand to add to your dinner salads during the coming weeks.

PER SERVING

Calories: 798; Fat: 71g; Sodium: 186mg; Carbohydrates: 38g; Protein: 15g; Fiber: 13g

BULGARIAN EGGPLANT, RED PEPPER, AND STEAK SALAD

SERVES 2

PREP TIME: 40 MINUTES / FINISH TIME: 5 MINUTES / TOTAL TIME: 45 MINUTES

GLUTEN-FREE

There is a traditional Bulgarian combination of roasted eggplant and red bell pepper that's usually served as a dip. This salad is a play on that dip; here, the eggplant is pan-cooked until golden brown and the pepper is roasted. They are then layered together over a bed of baby spinach and topped with sliced steak.

2 tablespoons extra-virgin olive oil

1 garlic clove, minced

1 rosemary sprig or 1 teaspoon dried rosemary

2 (4-ounce) flank steaks **P**

¼ cup walnuts **T**

1 red bell pepper **B**

Salt

Freshly ground black pepper

1 tablespoon unsalted butter

Grapeseed, canola, or extra-virgin olive oil, for pan-cooking

2 baby Japanese eggplants, cut into thin circles **V**

4 cups baby spinach **B**

¼ cup Honey-Mustard Vinaigrette (page 150)

1. Preheat the broiler.

2. In a resealable bag, combine the olive oil, garlic, rosemary, and flank steaks. Seal the bag and massage the meat to coat it in the marinade. Set aside and let marinate for about 15 minutes.

3. Toast the walnuts according to the instructions on page 15. Set aside.

4. Place the bell pepper on a baking sheet and place under the broiler for 5 to 10 minutes. Rotate the pepper every couple of minutes so it is evenly blackened on all sides. Transfer the pepper to a resealable bag. Let sit for about 5 minutes. Reduce the oven to 375°F.

5. Remove the steaks from the marinade (discarding the liquid) and season generously on both sides with salt and pepper.

6. Heat a large oven-safe skillet over high heat. When the pan is very hot, add the steaks and sear on both sides, about 2 minutes per side. Transfer the skillet to the oven and continue cooking the steaks for 10 minutes.

7. Remove the skillet from the oven and place back on the stove over medium-high heat. Add the butter to melt. Using a spoon, baste the steaks with the melted butter for 2 minutes. Remove the skillet from the heat, cover with aluminum foil, and let the steaks rest for 5 minutes before slicing against the grain into strips.

8. Once the bell pepper is cool enough to handle, peel the skin and remove the seeds. Cut the pepper lengthwise into strips.

9. Heat a very thin layer of oil in a large skillet or griddle over high heat. When hot, add the eggplant slices in a single layer and cook until golden brown on both sides, 1 to 2 minutes per side.

10. In a large bowl, toss the spinach with the vinaigrette. Divide the salad between two plates. Top with the steak strips, bell pepper strips, and eggplant slices. Garnish with the toasted walnuts. Serve warm.

INGREDIENT TIP: Eggplant is virtually all water. As a result, it is spongy, and acts as such when in the presence of liquid. The eggplant will immediately soak up any oil, so be mindful of fat content.

PER SERVING
Calories: 776; Fat: 62g; Sodium: 295mg; Carbohydrates: 24g; Protein: 37g; Fiber: 12g

FRISÉE, BACON, AND POACHED EGG SALAD (LYONNAISE SALAD)

SERVES 2

PREP TIME: 20 MINUTES / FINISH TIME: 5 MINUTES / TOTAL TIME: 25 MINUTES

GLUTEN-FREE, NUT-FREE, DAIRY-FREE

Breakfast for dinner. Dinner for breakfast. Sometimes you've just gotta flip the script. Here, bacon and eggs become a breakfast salad for dinner.

4 thick slices bacon T
4 large eggs P
4 cups frisée B
¼ cup Honey-Mustard Vinaigrette (page 150)
Salt
Freshly ground black pepper

1. In a large skillet over medium-high heat, cook the bacon until crispy, 5 to 8 minutes. Drain on a paper towel–lined plate. Chop the bacon into bite-size pieces.

2. Poach the eggs according to the instructions on page 14.

3. Toss the frisée with the vinaigrette in a large bowl.

4. Divide the salad between two bowls. Top with the bacon and place the poached eggs on top. Season with salt and pepper. Serve warm.

OPTIONAL TIP: To lighten up the salad and cut through the richness of the bacon and eggs, add fresh tomatoes or thinly sliced red onion.

PER SERVING

Calories: 537; Fat: 46g; Sodium: 1,130mg; Carbohydrates: 4g; Protein: 27g; Fiber: 0g

EGGPLANT-FETA SALAD *page 78*

CHAPTER 5

MIDDLE EASTERN– AND MEDITERRANEAN– INSPIRED SALADS

This chapter has a special place in my heart because I was born and spent my early childhood living in Israel. The dinner salads in this chapter are inspired by Middle Eastern, North African, and Mediterranean cuisines. While the recipes themselves are not traditional, the flavors are. Two of my favorites are the Eggplant-Feta Salad (page 78), where the eggplants act as salad bowls, and the Steak, Pomegranate, and Citrus Salad (page 85)—both feature staples of the region, with my spin on them.

CHERMOULA COUSCOUS AND SALMON SALAD

SERVES 2

PREP TIME: 35 MINUTES / FINISH TIME: 5 MINUTES / TOTAL TIME: 40 MINUTES

NUT-FREE

Pack your bags for Morocco and board the Marrakech Express. It's amazing how you don't need a passport to feel like you're thousands of miles away. This recipe is an ode to Morocco and all its rich flavor profiles. It's just what I look for in a satisfying, delicious dinner salad.

1 cup couscous **B**
2 (5-ounce) salmon fillets **P**
1 tablespoon extra-virgin olive oil, plus
    more for rubbing on the salmon
Salt
Freshly ground black pepper
1 medium onion or 2 large shallots **V**
1 tablespoon unsalted butter
1 teaspoon sugar
6 tablespoons Chermoula Dressing
    (page 165)
¼ cup packed fresh mint leaves,
    cut into thin strips **T**

1. Cook the couscous according to the instructions on page 13. Fluff the cooked couscous with a fork and set aside.

2. Rub the salmon fillets generously with olive oil, salt, and pepper. Pan-sear the fillets according to the instructions on page 15. Once cooked, transfer to a plate and flake the fish with a fork.

3. While the salmon is cooking, cut the onion into thin circles. Heat 1 tablespoon of olive oil and the butter in a large skillet over high heat. Once the butter has melted, add the onion, sprinkle with the sugar, and cook, stirring occasionally, until caramelized, about 10 minutes. (Sugar speeds the caramelization process.)

4. Add the couscous and flaked salmon to the caramelized onions and toss to combine.

5. Divide the salad between two plates. Drizzle with the dressing and garnish with the mint. Serve warm.

INGREDIENT TIP: It's impossible to talk about North African cuisine without talking about chermoula. It's one of the most common marinades in the region and has many variations. Although traditionally a marinade for seafood, it packs so much flavor that it can easily be used as the dressing for delicious weeknight salads. Some chermoula variations get more heat from ground chiles; others are a bit sweeter with cinnamon; some use fresh herbs such as parsley or mint, while still others include preserved lemons for sourness. Chermoula is usually made as a thick paste, and it is bright red because of the paprika and saffron.

PER SERVING

Calories: 664; Fat: 36g; Sodium: 156mg;
Carbohydrates: 51g; Protein: 32g; Fiber: 5g

MUJADARRA WITH CUMIN-MINT YOGURT DRESSING

SERVES 4

PREP TIME: 35 MINUTES / FINISH TIME: 5 MINUTES / TOTAL TIME: 40 MINUTES

VEGETARIAN, GLUTEN-FREE, NUT-FREE

A staple of the Middle East, mujadarra is a delicious combination of rice and lentils. When these two ingredients are eaten together, they make a complete protein. When mixed with sweet caramelized onions and the bright freshness of mint, along with a tangy, earthy dressing, the result is a satisfying dinner salad.

1 cup jasmine rice **B**

1 cup green lentils **P**

Salt

Freshly ground black pepper

2 tablespoons extra-virgin olive oil, divided

1 tablespoon unsalted butter

1 large onion, halved and cut into thin half-moons **V**

1 teaspoon sugar

¼ cup packed fresh mint leaves, cut into thin strips **T**

½ cup Cumin-Mint Yogurt Dressing (page 162)

1. Combine the rice and 2 cups of water in a large pot. Cook according to the instructions on page 14.

2. Cook the lentils according to the instructions on page 14. Season the lentils with salt and pepper.

3. While the rice and lentils are cooking, heat 1 tablespoon of olive oil and the butter in a large skillet over high heat. Once the butter has melted, add the onion, sprinkle with the sugar, and cook, stirring occasionally, until caramelized, about 10 minutes.

4. Reduce the heat to medium-high. Add the cooked rice and lentils to the skillet along with the remaining 1 tablespoon of olive oil, stirring to combine. Cook for about 3 minutes to let the flavors come together. Add the mint and toss to combine.

5. Divide the salad among four plates. Drizzle with the dressing and serve warm.

OPTIONAL TIP: This recipe packs a ton of protein between the lentils and the yogurt that's in the dressing. But if you're looking to get in a little extra protein, chickpeas complement the rest of the ingredients perfectly. Drain and rinse a 15-ounce can. Either pan-fry them along with some paprika and cumin, or dry roast them in the oven. They can be mixed in with the salad or used as a garnish.

SUBSTITUTION TIP: You can use another long-grain rice, such as basmati, instead of the jasmine rice.

PER SERVING

Calories: 469; Fat: 13g; Sodium: 105mg; Carbohydrates: 72g; Protein: 17g; Fiber: 18g

EGGPLANT-FETA SALAD

SERVES 2 OR 3

PREP TIME: 1 HOUR / FINISH TIME: 5 MINUTES / TOTAL TIME: 1 HOUR 5 MINUTES

VEGETARIAN

One of the most amazing eggplant dishes I've ever had was in Israel. It was a whole broiled eggplant topped with tahini, feta, and parsley. It was perfectly smoky from the char, creamy from the tahini, and tangy and salty from the feta. This is an attempt to re-create that dish I had in Kfar Saba, my hometown. And, of course, I make it with my twist on it.

2 large male eggplants
   (see Ingredient tip) V
Extra-virgin olive oil, for brushing
1 cup whole-wheat couscous B
Salt
Freshly ground black pepper
6 tablespoons Lemon-Tahini Dressing
   (page 158)
1 cup crumbled feta cheese P
1 cup loosely packed fresh parsley
   leaves, finely chopped V
Seeds from ½ pomegranate,
   for garnish (optional) T

1. Preheat the oven to 375°F. Position a rack in the middle of the oven and another closest to the broiler.

2. Poke holes in the eggplants using a fork or knife. This will let steam come out of them while they roast so they don't explode in the oven. Brush them lightly all over with olive oil. Place them on a baking sheet and roast on the middle rack for 30 minutes, rotating the baking sheet halfway through.

3. Switch the oven setting to broil and move the eggplants to the rack closest to the broiler. Broil for 20 minutes, rotating them every few minutes to make sure there's an even char on all sides. Once charred, let the eggplants sit for about 5 minutes to cool.

4. While the eggplants are broiling, cook the couscous according to the instructions on page 13. Fluff the cooked couscous with a fork.

5. Halve each eggplant lengthwise, keeping the end on and trying not to damage the skin, as it will serve as the salad bowl. Gently scoop out the eggplant flesh and place in a medium bowl. Season it generously with salt and pepper. Add the dressing and stir to combine.

6. Divide the couscous among the four pieces of eggplant skin. Top with the eggplant mixture and sprinkle with the feta, chopped parsley, and pomegranate seeds (if using). Serve warm.

INGREDIENT TIP: Yes, eggplants actually have a gender. This recipe calls for male eggplants because they tend to have fewer seeds than female eggplants. This makes for a gentler, less bitter taste. How do you spot a male or female eggplant? Look at the slit at the bottom. If it's deep and long, it's a girl. If it's shallow and round, it's a boy.

SHORTCUT TIP: Slash the cooking time of this recipe in half by grilling the eggplant. Not only does this cut the cooking time to just 10 minutes, it also creates a smokier, even more delicious flavor. Just make sure to poke holes in the eggplant and lightly brush it with olive oil, the same as you would if roasting and broiling.

PER SERVING

Calories: 656; Fat: 33g; Sodium: 683mg; Carbohydrates: 76g; Protein: 23g; Fiber: 18g

CARAMELIZED FIG AND PROSCIUTTO SALAD

SERVES 2

PREP TIME: 20 MINUTES / FINISH TIME: 5 MINUTES / TOTAL TIME: 25 MINUTES

GLUTEN-FREE, NUT-FREE

You can never go wrong with sweet and salty. The salt brings out the sweetness of ingredients while, simultaneously, the sweetness balances the astringency of the salt. It's yin and yang at the most basic level. I can't get enough of fresh figs when they're in season. Figs, prosciutto, goat cheese, and fresh mint is a divine, satisfying combination that will please and impress.

4 cups baby arugula B
½ cup packed fresh mint leaves, cut into thin strips T
¼ cup Date-Balsamic Vinaigrette (page 163)
8 to 10 fresh figs (about 1 cup) V
2 tablespoons unsalted butter
3 teaspoons sugar, divided
6 thin slices prosciutto (about 2 ounces) P
⅓ cup crumbled goat cheese (optional) B
Salt
Freshly ground black pepper

1. Place the arugula and mint in a large bowl. Drizzle with the vinaigrette and toss to combine.

2. Cut the figs lengthwise into thin slices.

3. In a large skillet over high heat, melt the butter. Add the fig strips in a single layer (they should not overlap) and sprinkle with 1½ teaspoons of sugar. Cook the figs without stirring them. After 5 minutes, flip them over and sprinkle with the remaining 1½ teaspoons of sugar. Continue to cook for 5 minutes, or until the figs are caramelized. Remove the skillet from the heat.

4. Divide the salad between two bowls or plates. Ribbon 3 slices of prosciutto onto each salad. Top with the caramelized figs and garnish with the goat cheese (if using). Season with salt and pepper. Serve while the figs are still warm or at room temperature.

INGREDIENT TIP: Figs are awesome. Have I mentioned how much I love fresh figs? They're gorgeous, nutritious, and sweet. In fact, the fig tree is a symbol of abundance, fertility, and sweetness. I'm proud to be from California, where we produce 98 percent of the U.S. supply of fresh figs.

SUBSTITUTION TIP: Salami is a great replacement for prosciutto.

PER SERVING

Calories: 613; Fat: 30g; Sodium: 201mg; Carbohydrates: 104g; Protein: 5g; Fiber: 14g

ZOODLE GREEK SALAD

SERVES 2

PREP TIME: 20 MINUTES / FINISH TIME: 5 MINUTES / TOTAL TIME: 25 MINUTES

VEGETARIAN, GLUTEN-FREE, NUT-FREE

Spiralizing fruits and veggies has really blown up. I'm all about it. It's a great way to sneak in healthy foods in a fun way. Plus, the spiral shape makes sauces and dressings stick better, so the vegetables are more flavorful and delicious. If you don't have a spiralizer, don't fret. You can use a vegetable peeler instead to shave the zucchini here so they look like little green ribbons.

2 large zucchinis **B**

1¼ cups cherry tomatoes, halved **V**

2 Persian cucumbers, halved lengthwise and cut into half-moons **V**

½ cup pitted Kalamata olives or other assorted pitted olives, halved **T**

¼ cup Lemon Vinaigrette (page 146)

Salt

Freshly ground black pepper

½ cup crumbled feta cheese **P**

OPTIONAL TIP: Greek salad has a lot of potential to be further bedazzled. Add pickled red onions, artichokes marinated in oil, red bell peppers, and/or grilled chicken to take it to the next level.

PER SERVING

Calories: 463; Fat: 37g; Sodium: 790mg; Carbohydrates: 29g; Protein: 12g; Fiber: 7g

1. Spiralize the zucchini into noodles (or zoodles), leaving the skin on. Alternatively, use a vegetable peeler to shave the zucchini into thin strips.

2. Combine the zucchini, tomatoes, cucumbers, and olives in a large bowl. Drizzle with the vinaigrette and toss to combine. Season with salt and pepper.

3. Divide the salad between two plates or bowls. Garnish with the feta and serve cold.

BULGUR, HALLOUMI, AND WATERMELON SALAD

SERVES 2
PREP TIME: 30 MINUTES / FINISH TIME: 5 MINUTES / TOTAL TIME: 35 MINUTES
VEGETARIAN, NUT-FREE

Turkey is high up on my travel list. When I visited Sydney, Australia, I was pleasantly surprised by the volume of Turkish food available. Halloumi cheese was literally everywhere and has quickly become one of my favorite ingredients! It is a perfect addition to this refreshing and healthy summer dinner salad.

1 cup bulgur wheat B
4 cups diced watermelon (about 1 ripe medium watermelon) V
1 tablespoon sugar
8 ounces halloumi or other grilling cheese P
2 tablespoons extra-virgin olive oil
¼ cup packed fresh mint leaves T
¼ cup Herb Vinaigrette (page 148)
Salt
Freshly ground black pepper

1. Cook the bulgur according to the instructions on page 13 (use 2½ cups of boiling water). Once cooked, fluff the bulgur with a fork. Set aside to cool.

2. Place the watermelon in a large bowl and sprinkle with the sugar.

3. Cut the halloumi into slices as thin as you can without ripping the cheese.

4. Heat the olive oil in a large skillet over high heat. When hot, add the halloumi in a single layer, making sure the slices do not overlap (you may need to cook the cheese in batches). Cook the halloumi until a nice sear appears on the cheese, about 2 minutes on the first side. Flip the slices over and continue cooking for about 1 minute. Transfer the cheese to a paper towel–lined plate and let cool.

5. Cut the halloumi into bite-size cubes.

6. Add the bulgur, mint leaves, and fried halloumi "croutons" to the bowl with the watermelon. Drizzle with the vinaigrette and toss to combine. Season with salt and pepper.

7. Divide the salad between two plates or bowls and serve cold.

INGREDIENT TIP: Halloumi is wild, so is it any wonder I love it so much? Its flavor is somewhere between mozzarella and feta. It's less salty and firmer than feta, and has a very high melting point, making it perfect for grilling or frying. It's becoming more common in grocery stores.

SUBSTITUTION TIP: If you can't find halloumi, use farmer's cheese instead.

PER SERVING
Calories: 928; Fat: 57g; Sodium: 1,375mg; Carbohydrates: 89g; Protein: 27g; Fiber: 16g

BROWN RICE, ROASTED KALE, AND HARISSA CHICKPEA SALAD

SERVES 3

PREP TIME: 30 MINUTES / FINISH TIME: 5 MINUTES / TOTAL TIME: 35 MINUTES

VEGAN, GLUTEN-FREE, NUT-FREE, DAIRY-FREE

I do love me some kale. It's delicious and highly nutritional—packed with tons of vitamins A and C. It's not just a super food, it's a superfood. In this dinner salad, I let the oven do all the work. This warm roasted kale and spiced chickpea salad will satisfy your tummy and is kind to your waistline.

1 cup brown rice B
1 head of kale, torn into
  bite-size pieces V
¼ cup extra-virgin olive oil
Salt
Freshly ground black pepper
1 (15-ounce) can chickpeas T
2 tablespoons harissa paste or
  1 tablespoon dry harissa seasoning,
  or to taste
6 tablespoons Lemon Vinaigrette
  (page 146)

1. Preheat the oven to 400°F.

2. Combine the rice and 2 cups of water in a large pot. Cook according to the instructions on page 14.

3. Arrange the kale pieces on a baking sheet. Toss with the olive oil and season with salt and pepper. Set aside.

4. Drain and rinse the chickpeas. Dry them with a paper towel. It's important they are fully dry or they won't get crispy when roasted. Place them on a separate baking sheet, toss with the harissa, and season with salt and pepper.

5. Place both baking sheets in the oven and roast the kale and chickpeas for about 20 minutes, turning the kale and stirring the chickpeas after about 10 minutes.

6. In a large bowl, combine the rice, kale, chickpeas, and vinaigrette. Gently toss to combine.

7. Divide the salad among three bowls and serve warm.

INGREDIENT TIP: Harissa is a North African hot, smoked chili paste. Depending on the spice blend, it can include cumin, red chile, crushed garlic, coriander, and lemon. It can be found in Middle Eastern groceries or specialty stores. Harissa can pack some massive heat depending on the blend, so adjust the amount you use according to your taste. If you're unable to find the paste or dry seasoning, you can substitute with another chili paste or chili blend.

PER SERVING

Calories: 985; Fat: 61g; Sodium: 1,190mg; Carbohydrates: 96g; Protein: 15g; Fiber: 11g

MEDITERRANEAN QUINOA-SALMON SALAD

SERVES 2

PREP TIME: 35 MINUTES / FINISH TIME: 5 MINUTES / TOTAL TIME: 40 MINUTES

GLUTEN-FREE, NUT-FREE

The Mediterranean diet is all about seafood, whole grains, and healthy fats. This salad is a dedication to that diet. Quinoa is traditionally a South American ingredient, but it translates well into recipes that call for rice, bulgur, or other grains. It absorbs the flavors of the other ingredients and has a wonderful chewy-crunchy texture. It's also packed with protein, making it more nutritious than other grains.

¾ cup quinoa **B**
2 (5-ounce) salmon fillets **P**
Salt
Freshly ground black pepper
2 large tomatoes, finely chopped **V**
½ small red onion, finely chopped **B**
½ cup crumbled feta cheese **T**
¼ cup Herb Vinaigrette (page 148)

1. Cook the quinoa according to the instructions on page 13. Once cooked, fluff the quinoa with a fork.

2. Season the salmon generously on both sides with the salt and pepper. Pan-sear it according to the instructions on page 15.

3. Transfer the cooked salmon to a cutting board and cut into bite-size pieces. Alternatively, keep the salmon fillets whole and serve them on top of the salad.

4. Place the quinoa, tomatoes, red onion, salmon (if it was cut into bite-size pieces), and feta in a large bowl. Season with a generous pinch of salt and pepper. Drizzle with the vinaigrette and toss to combine.

5. Divide the salad between two bowls. Serve warm or cold.

SUBSTITUTION TIP: For a cheaper and faster option, use canned salmon.

MAKE-AHEAD TIP: This salad tastes best if it's chilled overnight, as the quinoa really absorbs all the flavors. That makes this a great meal-prep-friendly salad that can be prepared the night before so you have a ready-made dinner the next evening—but only if you can keep yourself from eating it for lunch.

PER SERVING

Calories: 1,155; Fat: 57g; Sodium: 1,113mg; Carbohydrates: 105g; Protein: 54g; Fiber: 16g

STEAK, POMEGRANATE, AND CITRUS SALAD

SERVES 2

PREP TIME: 35 MINUTES / FINISH TIME: 5 MINUTES / TOTAL TIME: 40 MINUTES

GLUTEN-FREE, NUT-FREE

Fruit in salads adds a ton of fiber and flavor without too many calories. I love pomegranate seeds myself. The burst of flavor they provide always delights me no matter that I've eaten them countless times. The sweet and savory combination in play in this salad works really well, with the acidic grapefruit dressing binding it all together.

2 tablespoons extra-virgin olive oil
1 garlic clove, minced
1 rosemary sprig or 1 teaspoon dried rosemary
2 (4-ounce) flank steaks **P**
Salt
Freshly ground black pepper
1 cup baby arugula **B**
2 cups baby spinach **B**
1 cup spoon cabbage (optional) **B**
4 radishes, thinly sliced **B**
1 tablespoon unsalted butter
1 small grapefruit, peeled and cut into wedges **V**
Seeds of ½ small pomegranate **T**
¼ cup Charred Grapefruit Vinaigrette (page 160)

1. Preheat the oven to 375°F.

2. In a resealable bag, combine the olive oil, garlic, rosemary, and flank steaks. Seal the bag and massage the meat to coat it in the marinade. Set aside and let marinate for 15 minutes.

3. Remove the steaks from the marinade (discarding the liquid) and generously season on both sides with salt and pepper. Place a large oven-safe skillet over high heat. Once the skillet is very hot, add the steaks and sear on both sides, about 2 minutes per side. Transfer the skillet to the oven and continue cooking the steaks for 10 minutes.

4. Remove the skillet from the oven and place back on the stove over medium-high heat. Add the butter to melt. Using a spoon, baste the steaks with the melted butter for 2 minutes. Remove the skillet from the heat, cover it with aluminum foil, and let the steaks rest for 5 minutes.

5. While the steaks rest, place the arugula, spinach, spoon cabbage (if using), radishes, grapefruit wedges, and pomegranate seeds in a large bowl and toss to combine. Divide the salad between two bowls.

6. Slice the steak against the grain into strips. Add to the salad bowls and drizzle everything with the vinaigrette. Serve while the steak is warm.

INGREDIENT TIP: Keeping pomegranate seeds on hand is a great way to have ready-to-go salad toppings in no time.

PER SERVING

Calories: 658; Fat: 54g; Sodium: 216mg; Carbohydrates: 20g; Protein: 26g; Fiber: 2g

SHAKSHUKA AND COUSCOUS SALAD

SERVES 2

PREP TIME: 25 MINUTES / FINISH TIME: 5 MINUTES / TOTAL TIME: 30 MINUTES

VEGETARIAN, NUT-FREE

Brunch meets the Middle East. Shakshuka is a rustic, traditional North African dish typically served right out of the skillet. It is comprised of eggs slowly poached in a stew of peppers, tomatoes, and spices. Fresh bread is ripped and dipped straight into the skillet. Modern additions include feta cheese. Even more modern is taking those flavors and ingredients and turning them into a hearty dinner salad.

½ cup couscous **B**

3 tablespoons extra-virgin olive oil

½ teaspoon paprika

½ teaspoon ground cumin

2 cups cherry tomatoes, halved **V**

1 red or yellow bell pepper, cut into short matchsticks **V**

4 large eggs **P**

Salt

Freshly ground black pepper

¼ cup Herb Vinaigrette (page 148)

½ cup crumbled feta cheese **T**

1. Cook the couscous according to the instructions on page 13. Fluff the cooked couscous with a fork.

2. Heat the olive oil in a medium skillet over high heat. Once hot, add the paprika and cumin and cook just until aromatic, about 1 minute. Add the tomatoes and bell pepper. Cook, stirring occasionally, until the tomatoes have caramelized, 5 to 10 minutes.

3. Create four small wells in the tomato and pepper mixture. Crack 1 egg into each well. Reduce the heat to medium and cover the skillet with a lid. Poach the eggs for about 5 minutes, until the whites are set but the yolks are still runny.

4. Remove the lid and generously season the eggs and vegetables with salt and pepper.

5. Divide the couscous between two bowls. Divide the tomato and pepper mixture and the poached eggs between the bowls, being careful not to break the yolks. Drizzle with the vinaigrette and top with the feta. Serve warm.

OPTIONAL TIP: Adding a kick of heat goes a long way in this dish. Garnish each salad with a pinch of cayenne pepper or fresh jalapeño slices for added flavor. The natural sweetness of the cooked tomatoes will balance out the heat.

PER SERVING

Calories: 790; Fat: 57g; Sodium: 665mg; Carbohydrates: 49g; Protein: 26g; Fiber: 6g

CHICKEN GYRO SALAD

SERVES 4

PREP TIME: 35 MINUTES / FINISH TIME: 5 MINUTES / TOTAL TIME: 40 MINUTES

GLUTEN-FREE, NUT-FREE

Be a hero and make this gyro (pronounced "yee-ro" in Greek), or shawarma as it's known in the Middle East. It is the quintessential street food. Traditionally it's made with lamb that is slow-roasted on a vertical spit. When someone orders, the meat is shaved off. It's a delight to watch it done. I've deconstructed this street-food favorite, using chicken, into a delicious and healthy dinner salad. Sorry, no shaving needed.

1 pound chicken breast **P**
Salt
Freshly ground black pepper
1 tablespoon shawarma seasoning
2 tablespoons extra-virgin olive oil
7 or 8 cups shredded romaine lettuce **B**
2 Persian cucumbers, sliced **V**
2 cups cherry tomatoes, halved **V**
1 cup crumbled feta cheese **T**
6 tablespoons Dill, Lemon, and Garlic
    Sour Cream Dressing (page 159)

1. Cook the chicken according to the instructions on page 15. Use salt, pepper, and the shawarma seasoning to season the chicken and the olive oil to cook it.

2. Place the romaine lettuce, cucumbers, tomatoes, and feta in a large bowl and toss to combine.

3. Slice the chicken into bite-size strips.

4. Divide the salad among four bowls. Layer the chicken strips over the salad and drizzle it all with the dressing. Serve while the chicken is warm.

OPTIONAL TIP: Serve with pita chips for an extra crunch. If you have pita on hand, cut into wedges, drizzle with olive oil, and sprinkle with paprika, cumin, and/or za'atar. Bake in a preheated 400°F oven for 6 to 8 minutes, flipping the chips halfway through.

INGREDIENT TIP: Shawarma seasoning is generally a blend of coriander, allspice, cinnamon, cumin, ginger, turmeric, salt, and black pepper. It can be found in Middle Eastern groceries or specialty markets.

PER SERVING

Calories: 510; Fat: 28g; Sodium: 788mg; Carbohydrates: 23g; Protein: 45g; Fiber: 4g

DECONSTRUCTED FALAFEL SALAD

SERVES 3 OR 4

PREP TIME: 35 MINUTES / FINISH TIME: 5 MINUTES / TOTAL TIME: 40 MINUTES

VEGETARIAN, DAIRY-FREE

Walk down any major street in Israel—and secondary streets, too—and you're likely to find a falafel stand. You'll get fresh pita stuffed with deep-fried falafel balls, pickled cabbage, hummus, tahini, pickles, and other toppings. This dinner salad is a cross between a tabouleh bulgur wheat salad and a falafel sandwich. Pickles in a salad? The Middle Eastern kind are cold, salty, a deep-green color, and just perfect. They add a crisp, salty bite that's perfect with warm, spicy chickpeas.

1 cup bulgur wheat B
2 tablespoons extra-virgin olive oil
1 (15-ounce) can chickpeas, drained and rinsed P
1½ teaspoons shawarma seasoning
1 cup tightly packed fresh parsley leaves, roughly chopped V
1 cup cherry tomatoes, halved V
4 large Mediterranean pickles, diced T
Salt
Freshly ground black pepper
6 tablespoons Lemon-Tahini Dressing (page 158)

1. Cook the bulgur according to the instructions on page 13. Once cooked, fluff it with a fork.

2. Heat the olive oil in a large skillet over high heat. When hot, add the chickpeas and season with the shawarma seasoning. Cook, stirring occasionally, until the chickpeas are crispy, about 10 minutes.

3. Place the parsley, tomatoes, and pickles in a large bowl and toss to combine. Add the bulgur wheat and chickpeas and toss to combine. Season with salt and pepper.

4. Divide the salad among three or four bowls. Drizzle with the dressing and serve at room temperature.

INGREDIENT TIP: Bulgur wheat is a healthy whole grain mainly eaten in the Middle East. It is often confused with rice, couscous, or cracked wheat, but it has its own unique profile. It has a light, nutty flavor and is cooked similarly to rice. It's extremely healthy and can be found in most supermarkets.

PER SERVING
Calories: 644; Fat: 29g; Sodium: 2,792mg; Carbohydrates: 87g; Protein: 20g; Fiber: 22g

TOMATO, CHICKPEA, CUCUMBER, AND SALMON SALAD

SERVES 2

PREP TIME: 35 MINUTES / FINISH TIME: 5 MINUTES / TOTAL TIME: 40 MINUTES

GLUTEN-FREE, NUT-FREE

This dinner salad is a convergence of Mediterranean flavors that equals a perfect combination of sweet, salty, and savory. I like to use canned salmon in this salad, but it can just as easily be made with salmon fillets. Pan-sear them according to the instructions on page 15, flake the cooked salmon with a fork, and add to the salad. This salad is also a good way to use up leftover salmon from the previous night's dinner.

1 (15-ounce) can chickpeas **B**
2 medium tomatoes, chopped **V**
2 Persian cucumbers, halved lengthwise and cut into half-moons **V**
½ small red onion, finely chopped **B**
2 (4-ounce) cans salmon **P**
Salt
Freshly ground black pepper
¼ cup Herb Vinaigrette (page 148)

1. Drain and rinse the chickpeas. Place them in a large bowl along with the tomatoes, cucumbers, and red onion.

2. Drain the salmon and flake it with a fork to separate the pieces. Add to the bowl with the chickpeas and vegetables. Season the salad with a generous pinch of salt and pepper and toss to combine.

3. Drizzle the salad with the vinaigrette and toss to combine.

4. Divide the salad between two bowls or plates. Serve cold.

INGREDIENT TIP: Holy chickpea! Or is it a garbanzo bean? Garbanzo beans and chickpeas are exactly the same thing. *Chickpea* is the more common term, used worldwide, but you'll see *garbanzo bean* pop up on occasion, especially on American menus.

PER SERVING

Calories: 664; Fat: 27g; Sodium: 867mg; Carbohydrates: 74g; Protein: 27g; Fiber: 15g

WARM COUSCOUS SALAD WITH LAMB, OLIVES, AND FETA

SERVES 3 OR 4

PREP TIME: 35 MINUTES / FINISH TIME: 5 MINUTES / TOTAL TIME: 40 MINUTES

NUT-FREE

This salad is an ode to one of my favorite appetizers: warm spiced olives. Rosemary and orange with high-quality Mediterranean olives, slowly cooked together, is a match made in heaven. Don't leave a bowl of them in front of me—I can't resist them. To create this salad, add some couscous, lamb, and feta and you're in for a satisfying dinner.

1 cup couscous **B**
1 tablespoon extra-virgin olive oil
½ tablespoon shawarma seasoning
1 pound ground lamb **P**
Salt
Freshly ground black pepper
1 cup pitted olives, roughly chopped **T**
1 cup loosely packed fresh parsley leaves, roughly chopped **V**
6 tablespoons Honey-Orange Vinaigrette (page 151)
¾ cup crumbled feta cheese **B**

1. Cook the couscous according to the instructions on page 13. Fluff the cooked couscous with a fork.

2. In a medium skillet over high heat, add the olive oil. When hot, add the shawarma seasoning and toast for about 1 minute, or until fragrant. Add the ground lamb and reduce the heat to medium-high. Season the lamb with salt and pepper. With a wooden spoon, break apart the lamb into crumbles. Cook, stirring occasionally, until browned and cooked through, about 10 minutes.

3. In a large bowl, combine the couscous, ground lamb, olives, and parsley. Drizzle with the vinaigrette and toss to combine.

4. Divide the salad among three or four bowls. Top with the feta. Serve warm.

TECHNIQUE TIP: "Frying" spices in oil as opposed to adding them to food before or during cooking adds a ton of flavor. The spices toast and release into the oil, amplifying the flavors. This is a great trick to get a ton of extra flavor without adding extra calories to your meals.

PER SERVING
Calories: 1,031; Fat: 73g; Sodium: 1,499mg; Carbohydrates: 56g; Protein: 40g; Fiber: 7g

SARDINE, BLOOD ORANGE, AND FENNEL SALAD

SERVES 2

PREP TIME: 10 MINUTES / FINISH TIME: 5 MINUTES / TOTAL TIME: 15 MINUTES

GLUTEN-FREE, NUT-FREE, DAIRY-FREE

Not to put my dad on blast, but one of my strongest memories of childhood was when he would eat canned sardines in oil. I could smell his breath from a mile away, but I'd take stinky breath any day for the deliciousness of this ingredient.

1 large fennel bulb **B**
1 (4-ounce) can sardines packed in oil, preferably boneless and skinless **P**
Juice of 1 lemon
2 large blood oranges **V**
½ teaspoon red pepper flakes (optional)

1. Shave the fennel into a large bowl using a vegetable peeler or mandoline.

2. Drain the sardines, reserving the oil in a small bowl.

3. Whisk the lemon juice into the sardine oil.

4. Peel the blood oranges and cut them into wedges or slice into half-moons. Reserve any juice from the oranges and whisk it into the lemon oil.

5. Add the oranges and sardines to the fennel. Drizzle the salad with about 3 tablespoons of the oil mixture and toss to combine.

6. Divide the salad between two plates. Serve cold, garnished with the red pepper flakes (if using).

PER SERVING

Calories: 338; Fat: 17g; Sodium: 486mg; Carbohydrates: 31g; Protein: 19g; Fiber: 9g

MUHAMMARA STEAK SALAD
(PEPPER, WALNUT, AND STEAK SALAD)

SERVES 1

PREP TIME: 30 MINUTES / FINISH TIME: 5 MINUTES / TOTAL TIME: 35 MINUTES

GLUTEN-FREE

Muhammara is an out-of-this-world puréed dip made from roasted red peppers and walnuts. This salad is a deconstructed interpretation of the dip, made with steak, roasted red peppers, and walnuts. For extra crunch and maybe a few extra carbs, serve the salad with some homemade pita chips.

2 tablespoons extra-virgin olive oil
1 garlic clove, minced
1 rosemary sprig or 1 teaspoon dried
    rosemary
1 (4-ounce) flank steak P
1 red bell pepper V
Salt
Freshly ground black pepper
1 tablespoon unsalted butter
2 cups baby spinach B
2 tablespoons Lemon Vinaigrette
    (page 146)
¼ cup pomegranate seeds B
¼ cup walnuts T

1. Preheat the broiler.

2. In a resealable bag, combine the olive oil, garlic, rosemary, and flank steak. Seal the bag and massage the meat to cover it in the marinade. Set aside and marinate for 15 minutes.

3. Place the bell pepper on a baking sheet and place it under the broiler for 5 to 10 minutes. Rotate the pepper every couple of minutes while it broils so it is evenly blackened on all sides. Transfer the charred pepper to a plastic bag and seal it. Let it sit for about 5 minutes.

4. Reduce the oven to 375°F.

5. Remove the steak from the marinade (discarding the liquid) and season generously on both sides with salt and pepper. Place an oven-safe medium skillet over high heat. When it is very hot, add the steak and sear on both sides, about 2 minutes per side. Transfer the skillet to the oven and continue to cook for 10 minutes.

6. Remove the skillet from the oven and place back on the stove over medium-high heat. Add the butter to melt. Using a spoon, baste the steak with the melted butter for 2 minutes. Remove the skillet from the heat, cover with aluminum foil, and let the steak rest for 5 minutes before slicing it against the grain into strips.

7. Once the pepper is cool enough to hand, peel the skin and remove the seeds. Slice the pepper into strips.

8. In a medium bowl, toss the spinach with the vinaigrette. Top with the steak and pepper strips. Garnish the salad with the pomegranate seeds and walnuts. Serve warm.

TECHNIQUE TIP: Broiling red peppers infuses them with a smoky, warm flavor. Baking involves using hot air, whereas broiling involves using infrared radiation, creating a nice char. Placing the still-hot charred peppers into a tightly sealed plastic bag steams them, which gets the skin very soft and loose, making it easy to remove with no fuss.

PER SERVING
Calories: 917; Fat: 88g; Sodium: 364mg; Carbohydrates: 16g; Protein: 32g; Fiber: 5g

ANTIPASTO SALAD

The traditional antipasto platter usually includes olives, anchovies, cheeses, and meats. It's served as an appetizer, usually family-style, in most Italian restaurants and certainly in most Italian homes. I can and have made a meal of it, so it was only natural to turn it into a dinner salad. Salty, fatty salami is paired with creamy mozzarella, sweet cherry tomatoes, and artichokes to make a rich and satisfying salad.

3 cups arugula B

6 tablespoons Pesto Dressing
   (page 155)

4 ounces salami slices, cut into
   thin strips P

3 ounces marinated mini mozzarella balls,
   quartered (see Optional tip) B

1 cup cherry tomatoes, halved V

½ cup drained canned artichokes
   (in water or oil), diced V

1. In a large bowl, toss the arugula with
   the dressing.

2. Add the salami, mozzarella, tomatoes,
   and artichokes to the dressed arugula.

3. Divide the salad between two plates.
   Serve cold.

OPTIONAL TIP: Mozzarella is a blank-canvas type of cheese, meaning it can really take on a lot of different flavors. A great way to easily infuse it with tons of flavor is to take store-bought plain mini mozzarella balls, drain the water, and fill the container with extra-virgin olive oil. Add red pepper flakes, crushed garlic, and/or dried Italian herbs to infuse the oil and mozzarella. This sits well in the refrigerator and is an easy way to elevate this salad.

PER SERVING

Calories: 501; Fat: 44g; Sodium: 921mg; Carbohydrates: 11g; Protein: 13g; Fiber: 1g

BALELA SALAD (THREE-BEAN SALAD)

SERVES 4

PREP TIME: 5 MINUTES / FINISH TIME: 5 MINUTES / TOTAL TIME: 10 MINUTES

VEGAN, GLUTEN-FREE, NUT-FREE, DAIRY-FREE

I first came upon this Mediterranean-style bean salad due to an accidental purchase at Trader Joe's, and I've been obsessed with it ever since. The acidity of the vinaigrette cuts through the rich, fibrous content of the beans, and the jalapeño elevates the flavor and gives it a nice, subtle kick of heat. As much as I love that Trader Joe's version, homemade is always better, and so is this Balela salad, in my humble opinion.

1 (15-ounce) can chickpeas **B**
1 (15-ounce) can black beans **P**
1 (15-ounce) can kidney beans **B**
1 medium red onion, finely chopped **B**
1 large jalapeño pepper, minced **T**
2 garlic cloves, minced
Ground cumin, for seasoning
Salt
Freshly ground black pepper
½ cup Herb Vinaigrette (page 148)

1. Drain and rinse the chickpeas, black beans, and kidney beans. Place them in a large glass bowl.

2. Stir the red onion, jalapeño, and garlic into the beans. Season the salad with cumin, salt, and pepper. Add the vinaigrette and toss to combine.

3. For the ideal flavor, refrigerate the salad for at least 30 minutes before dividing among four plates and serving.

LEFTOVER TIP: Transform leftover Balela salad into tasty fritters. In a food processor, blend the bean salad into a paste. Add an egg and bread crumbs to help bind the bean paste. Shape into patties and pan-fry in canola or extra-virgin olive oil. Fry eggs in the residual oil in the pan and place on top of the fritters.

PER SERVING

Calories: 470; Fat: 19g; Sodium: 747mg; Carbohydrates: 61g; Protein: 17g; Fiber: 16g

TUNA AND CANNELLINI BEAN SALAD

SERVES 2

PREP TIME: 5 MINUTES / FINISH TIME: 5 MINUTES / TOTAL TIME: 10 MINUTES

GLUTEN-FREE, NUT-FREE, DAIRY-FREE

Cannellini beans paired with tuna make for a perfect balance of fiber and protein. The Mediterranean diet is all about healthy fats and proteins, and this salad fits right into the equation. All the better, the salad makes for a hearty and satisfying dinner. You can even turn it into a burger (see Optional tip).

1 (15-ounce) can cannellini beans, drained and rinsed **B**

1 cup packed fresh parsley leaves, finely chopped **V**

2 (4-ounce) cans chunk light tuna packed in water, drained **P**

2 garlic cloves, minced

Grated zest and juice of 1 lemon

¼ cup extra-virgin olive oil

Salt

Freshly ground black pepper

1. Combine the beans, parsley, tuna, garlic, lemon zest and juice, and olive oil in a medium bowl. Season with salt and pepper.

2. Divide the salad between two bowls. Serve cold or at room temperature.

OPTIONAL TIP: Make cannellini bean tuna burgers instead! Pulse the beans in a food processor, then place in a bowl with the tuna, garlic, lemon zest and juice, and parsley. Stir in ¼ cup of mayonnaise and ¼ cup of bread crumbs to help bind the mixture. Form into patties and pan-fry in extra-virgin olive oil. Serve the burgers on a whole-wheat bun for a protein-and-fiber-packed dinner.

PER SERVING

Calories: 572; Fat: 28g; Sodium: 1,357mg; Carbohydrates: 41g; Protein: 41g; Fiber: 15g

CAPRESE PASTA SALAD

SERVES 2

PREP TIME: 10 MINUTES / FINISH TIME: 5 MINUTES / TOTAL TIME: 15 MINUTES

VEGETARIAN, NUT-FREE

Of all the pastas, orzo is in my top five. I love it so much, I even convinced a friend to name her dog Orzo. This salad is an ode to orzo—more so the pasta than the dog. Caprese is a classic Italian salad—the combination of tomato, mozzarella, and basil will never get old—and by serving it over orzo, it becomes a dinner pasta salad sure to satisfy.

⅔ cup orzo pasta **B**
1½ teaspoons extra-virgin olive oil
⅓ cup panko bread crumbs
3 ounces fresh marinated mini mozzarella cheese balls, quartered (page 94) **P**
1 cup cherry tomatoes, quartered **V**
½ cup packed fresh basil leaves, cut into thin strips **T**
¼ cup Pesto Dressing (page 155)
Freshly ground black pepper

1. Bring a large pot of salted water to a boil and add a drop of oil to prevent the pasta from sticking. Add the orzo and cook until al dente, about 8 minutes. Drain and rinse the orzo with cold water to stop the cooking process.

2. While the pasta cooks, heat the olive oil in a small skillet over high heat. When hot, add the panko and toast until all the oil is absorbed and the bread crumbs have browned, about 4 minutes.

3. Place the orzo in a large bowl. Add the mozzarella, tomatoes, basil, and dressing and toss to combine.

4. Divide the pasta salad between two bowls. Garnish with the toasted bread crumbs. Serve warm or cold.

INGREDIENT TIP: Even though most pastas are made from the same exact ingredients, they taste different in various dishes because of their ability to absorb sauces. Since orzo is small, it's great for absorbing whatever sauce goes on it.

PER SERVING

Calories: 564; Fat: 30g; Sodium: 488mg; Carbohydrates: 44g; Protein: 19g; Fiber: 2g

MANGO SHRIMP AND RICE CEVICHE SALAD *page 115*

CHAPTER 6

LATIN AMERICAN-INSPIRED SALADS

The salads in this chapter include recipes inspired by Latin American foods: mangos, ubiquitous in Caribbean cuisine; Brazilian hearts of palm; and elote (grilled corn on the cob with mayo and cheese) from Mexico, to name a few. The flavors are complex and comforting. Try the Tequila Orange Chicken and Quinoa Salad (page 113) for a marriage of flavors and cultures—quinoa is a superfood staple of Peru coupled with Mexico's best loved spirit. Or, for a bold taste of Argentina, try the Arugula, Bean, Corn, and Chimichurri Steak Salad (page 110).

AVOCADO, MANGO, AND CUCUMBER SALAD

SERVES 3

PREP TIME: 5 MINUTES / FINISH TIME: 5 MINUTES / TOTAL TIME: 10 MINUTES

VEGETARIAN, GLUTEN-FREE, NUT-FREE

Creamy avocado, sweet mango, earthy black beans, crisp cucumber, salty queso fresco, and tangy dressing all marry well to create an ultimate salad that's satisfying and can be put together in no time. Open a can of beans, take a few minutes to cube the mango and slice the cucumbers, toss with dressing, and dinner is served. Yet this salad is as bold in flavor as it is skimpy on prep time.

1 (15-ounce) can black beans, drained and rinsed **B**

1 medium avocado, cubed **B**

1 large mango, cubed **V**

2 Persian cucumbers, halved lengthwise cut into half-moons **V**

6 tablespoons Tajín-Citrus Vinaigrette (page 149)

Salt

Freshly ground black pepper

¾ cup crumbled queso fresco **T**

INGREDIENT TIP: Tajín is something you *must* have in your pantry. It's a tangy seasoning made of chili powder and lime, and it is heavenly on top of mango, watermelon, elote (Mexican grilled corn on the cob), and so much more.

PER SERVING

Calories: 585; Fat: 37g; Sodium: 742mg; Carbohydrates: 58g; Protein: 18g; Fiber: 15g

1. Place the beans, avocado, mango, and cucumbers in a medium bowl. Add the vinaigrette and toss to combine. Season the salad with salt and pepper.

2. Divide the salad among three bowls. Garnish with the queso fresco. Serve cold.

BEER-BATTERED COD AND PURPLE CABBAGE SALAD

SERVES 2

PREP TIME: 20 MINUTES / FINISH TIME: 5 MINUTES / TOTAL TIME: 25 MINUTES

NUT-FREE

Tender fried cod, earthy purple cabbage, sweet corn, crunchy tortilla strips, and Creamy Chipotle Dressing (page 156) mean you've got sweet, salty, crunchy, and spicy all in one go. That hits all the flavors and textures I enjoy in a fish taco. And as much as I love fish tacos, I don't always like the mess I make eating them. So skip the tacos and make this salad instead.

½ cup all-purpose flour
½ cup beer, preferably light
Salt
Freshly ground black pepper
¼ cup grapeseed, vegetable, or canola oil
2 (4-ounce) cod fillets P
4 cups shredded purple cabbage B
1 cup drained canned sweet corn V
2 radishes, thinly sliced B
1 cup crunchy tortilla strips T
¼ cup Creamy Chipotle Dressing (page 156)

1. In a small bowl, whisk together the flour and beer. The consistency should be thick but still runny. Adjust with more flour or beer as necessary. Generously season the batter with salt and pepper.

2. Heat the oil in a medium skillet over high heat. Once the oil is hot, dip the cod fillets one by one in the beer batter to coat and add to the skillet. Fry the cod for about 5 minutes per side, or until golden brown and cooked through. Transfer to a paper towel-lined plate and season with salt.

3. Place the cabbage, corn, radishes, and tortilla strips in a large bowl. Drizzle with the dressing and toss to combine.

4. Divide the salad between two plates. Top each with a fried cod fillet. Serve warm.

INGREDIENT TIP: Beer isn't just for drinking! It has become a popular cooking ingredient because its carbonation helps tenderize meat or fish, and it is a great emulsifier for flour-based batters.

PER SERVING

Calories: 804; Fat: 43g; Sodium: 572mg; Carbohydrates: 71g; Protein: 32g; Fiber: 8g

BRAZILIAN HEARTS OF PALM, EGG, AND AVOCADO SALAD

SERVES 2

PREP TIME: 20 MINUTES / FINISH TIME: 5 MINUTES / TOTAL TIME: 25 MINUTES

VEGETARIAN, GLUTEN-FREE, NUT-FREE, DAIRY-FREE

This salad will make you want to do the samba! If you like artichokes, odds are you'll love hearts of palm, although they aren't related even a little bit. They're similar in texture, but flavor-wise hearts of palm are slightly salty compared to the milder, slightly sweeter taste of artichokes. Hearts of palm go great in both savory and sweet salads. This one is creamy, earthy, rich, and super quick and simple to make.

1 (14-ounce) can hearts of palm, drained B
1 cup cherry tomatoes, halved V
½ cup fresh parsley, roughly chopped T
2 large eggs P
1 large ripe avocado, diced
1 tablespoon pickled red onions (page 13), finely chopped B
¼ cup mayonnaise
Juice of ½ lime
Salt
Freshly ground black pepper

INGREDIENT TIP: Hearts of palm grow within certain types of palm trees. Although the French are the largest consumer of hearts of palm, the vegetable is actually native to parts of South America and the South Pacific—that's where you find palm trees after all.

PER SERVING
Calories: 181; Fat: 11g; Sodium: 867mg; Carbohydrates: 16g; Protein: 9g; Fiber: 5g

1. Cut the hearts of palm crosswise into ¼-inch-thick slices. Place in a medium bowl with the tomatoes and parsley.

2. Hard-boil the eggs according to the instructions on page 14. Peel and dice the eggs.

3. Add the eggs, avocado, and pickled red onions to the bowl with the vegetables. Add the mayonnaise and lime juice, and stir to combine. Season with salt and pepper.

4. Divide the salad between two bowls. Serve at room temperature.

CHARRED POBLANO, CORN, AND WILD RICE SALAD

SERVES 4

PREP TIME: 30 MINUTES / FINISH TIME: 5 MINUTES / TOTAL TIME: 35 MINUTES

VEGAN, GLUTEN-FREE, NUT-FREE, DAIRY-FREE

When I think of poblano chiles, I think of the Sargento/Food Network competition I entered that got me two minutes of television fame. I had to create and photograph a dish that included poblano chiles, chicken thighs, tortillas, and Sargento 4 Cheese Mexican blend. That was my first time ever using poblanos, and definitely not my last.

1 cup wild rice B
2 ears corn B
2 large poblano chiles V
1 cup cherry tomatoes, halved V
½ cup fresh cilantro, coarsely chopped T
Salt
Freshly ground black pepper
½ cup Cilantro-Lime Dressing (page 152)

1. Preheat the broiler.

2. Cook the wild rice according to the instructions on page 14.

3. Bring a large pot of water to a rolling boil. Add the corn, cover the pot with a lid, and boil the corn for 5 minutes. Drain.

4. Place the corn and poblano chiles on a baking sheet. Place under the broiler for about 10 minutes, rotating the corn and chiles every couple of minutes to get an even char on all sides. Set the corn aside to cool.

5. Place the chiles in a large resealable bag and seal. Let sit for about 5 minutes to steam and cool down. Once cool enough to handle, remove and discard the peel and seeds. Cut the chiles into bite-size pieces and place in a medium bowl.

6. Stand the corn ears upright on a cutting board and use a sharp knife to cut the kernels off the cobs. Add the kernels to the bowl with the chiles.

7. Add the rice, tomatoes, and cilantro to the bowl and season with salt and pepper. Drizzle with the dressing and toss to combine.

8. Divide the salad among four plates, and serve warm or at room temperature.

INGREDIENT TIP: Poblano chiles are absolutely delicious. Their thick skin and mild heat make them perfect for stuffing or as a complement to any Mexican dish. They are often mislabeled as pasilla chiles, which are actually dried poblano chiles. My favorite way to use poblanos: in the Roasted Poblano Crema (page 161), of course. It makes for an incredible dip, sauce, and salad dressing.

SUBSTITUTION TIP: You can use bell peppers in place of poblanos, especially if you have bell peppers that need to be used up. The flavor profile of the salad changes, but it's just as delicious.

PER SERVING

Calories: 416; Fat: 22g; Sodium: 73mg; Carbohydrates: 49g; Protein: 9g; Fiber: 7g

SALMON PICO DE GALLO SALAD

SERVES 3 TO 4

PREP TIME: 10 MINUTES / FINISH TIME: 5 MINUTES / TOTAL TIME: 15 MINUTES

GLUTEN-FREE, NUT-FREE, DAIRY-FREE

This dinner salad is vibrant, healthy, filling, and ready in just minutes. It's also light enough that you won't be ready for a nap after eating. Pico de gallo, also known as salsa fresca, is a simple salad of tomatoes, onions, and cilantro. This salad takes pico de gallo to the next level by adding black beans and salmon. The result is a balanced, well-rounded, quick weeknight meal.

2 (6-ounce) cans salmon, drained **P**

1 (15-ounce) can black beans, drained and rinsed **B**

3 medium tomatoes on the vine or 4 Roma tomatoes, diced **V**

1 small onion or 1 large shallot, finely chopped **B**

½ cup loosely packed fresh cilantro leaves, coarsely chopped **T**

6 tablespoons Cilantro-Lime Dressing (page 152)

Salt

Freshly ground black pepper

OPTIONAL TIP: For extra heat and flavor, finely mince a jalapeño pepper or serrano chile. For a fresher salad, use fresh salmon fillets: Pan-sear them according to the instructions on page 15, then flake with a fork and add to the black beans and pico de gallo.

PER SERVING

Calories: 572; Fat: 31g; Sodium: 1,132mg; Carbohydrates: 31g; Protein: 40g; Fiber: 13g

1. Place the salmon, beans, tomatoes, onion, and cilantro in a medium bowl. Drizzle with the dressing and toss to combine. Season with salt and pepper.

2. Divide the salad between three or four plates. Serve cold.

STEAK AND ORANGE SALAD

SERVES 1

PREP TIME: 30 MINUTES / FINISH TIME: 5 MINUTES / TOTAL TIME: 35 MINUTES

GLUTEN-FREE, NUT-FREE

Steak and citrus is one of my favorite combinations. Steak is fatty, meaty, and rich, while citrus is vibrant, acidic, and sweet. This salad combines steak, orange, fresh mint, pickled red onions, and cotija cheese for maximum flavor.

2 tablespoons extra-virgin olive oil

1 garlic clove, minced

1 rosemary sprig or 1 teaspoon
   dried rosemary

1 (4-ounce) flank steak **P**

1 orange, cut into wedges **B**

¼ cup loosely packed fresh mint leaves,
   cut into thin strips **V**

2 tablespoons pickled red onions
   (page 13) or diced red onions **B**

Salt

Freshly ground black pepper

1 tablespoon unsalted butter

2 tablespoons Honey-Orange Vinaigrette
   (page 151)

¼ cup crumbled cotija cheese
   or queso fresco **T**

1. Preheat the oven to 375°F.

2. In a resealable bag, combine the olive oil, garlic, rosemary, and flank steak. Seal the bag and massage the meat to cover it in the marinade. Set aside to marinate for 15 minutes.

3. Arrange the orange wedges, mint, and red onions on a plate.

4. Remove the steak from the marinade (discarding the liquid) and season generously on both sides with salt and pepper. Place an oven-safe medium skillet over high heat. Once it is very hot, add the steak and sear on both sides, about 2 minutes per side. Transfer the skillet to the oven and continue cooking for 10 minutes.

5. Remove the skillet from the oven and place back on the stove over medium-high heat. Add the butter to melt. Using a spoon, baste the steak with the melted butter for 2 minutes. Remove the skillet from the heat, cover with aluminum foil, and let the steak rest for 5 minutes before slicing against the grain into strips.

6. Place the steak over the salad and drizzle with the vinaigrette. Top with the cotija cheese. Serve while steak is warm.

SUBSTITUTION TIP: Not in the mood for steak? Use shrimp or tofu. The citrus and mint in the salad go well with each of these proteins.

PER SERVING

Calories: 880; Fat: 82g; Sodium: 740mg; Carbohydrates: 30g; Protein: 33g; Fiber: 5g

LOADED ELOTE GUACAMOLE SALAD

SERVES 2

PREP TIME: 30 MINUTES / FINISH TIME: 5 MINUTES / TOTAL TIME: 35 MINUTES

VEGETARIAN, GLUTEN-FREE, NUT-FREE

Elotes (pronounced ehhh-lo-tess) are a Mexican-street-food favorite—grilled corn on the cob, smothered in creamy crema and sprinkled with cotija cheese or queso fresco, fresh cilantro, and Tajín (chili-lime powder). To make this an amazing and delicious dinner salad, I've combined it with avocado and hard-boiled eggs.

Salt
2 ears corn **V**
2 large eggs **P**
1 large, ripe avocado, halved and pitted **B**
½ cup loosely packed fresh cilantro leaves, finely chopped **B**
Juice of ½ lime
½ teaspoon Tajín (optional)
¼ cup cotija cheese **T**

1. Preheat the broiler.

2. Bring a large pot of water to a rolling boil and add a pinch of salt and the corn. Cover the pot with a lid and let the corn boil for 5 minutes. Drain.

3. Place the corn ears on a baking sheet and broil for about 10 minutes, rotating the ears every couple of minutes, until slightly charred on all sides.

4. When the corn is cool enough to handle, stand the ears upright on a cutting board and use a sharp knife to cut the kernels off the cobs.

5. Hard-boil the eggs according to the instructions on page 14. Peel and dice. Place in a medium bowl.

6. Scoop the avocado into the bowl with the eggs. Add the cilantro, lime juice, and Tajín (if using). Using the back of a fork, lightly mash the ingredients together. Mix in the corn and cotija cheese.

7. Divide the salad between two plates. Serve at room temperature.

PER SERVING

Calories: 464; Fat: 30g; Sodium: 388mg; Carbohydrates: 41g; Protein: 16g; Fiber: 11g

MEXICAN STEAK AND WATERMELON SALAD

SERVES 1

PREP TIME: 30 MINUTES / FINISH TIME: 5 MINUTES / TOTAL TIME: 35 MINUTES

GLUTEN-FREE, NUT-FREE

If you love summer, you'll love this salad. After all, what tastes more like summer than cold, sliced, fresh watermelon? Combine it with savory steak, crumbly, salty cotija cheese, fresh mint leaves, and tangy Tajín dressing and, well, you're in for a satisfying summer salad. Why not go all the way and grill the steak on the barbecue?

2 tablespoons extra-virgin olive oil

1 garlic clove, minced

1 fresh rosemary sprig or 1 teaspoon dried rosemary

1 (4-ounce) flank steak P

Salt

Freshly ground black pepper

1 tablespoon unsalted butter

1 cup diced watermelon B

¼ cup crumbled cotija cheese B

¼ cup loosely packed fresh mint leaves, thinly sliced T

Tajín-Citrus Vinaigrette (page 149)

1. Preheat the oven to 375°F.

2. In a resealable bag, combine the olive oil, garlic, rosemary, and flank steak. Seal the bag and massage the meat to coat it in the marinade. Set aside to marinate for 15 minutes.

3. Remove the steak from the marinade (discarding the liquid) and season generously on both sides with salt and pepper. Place an oven-safe medium skillet over high heat. When the pan is very hot, add the steak and sear on both sides, about 2 minutes per side. Transfer the skillet to the oven and continue cooking the steak for 10 minutes.

4. Remove the skillet from the oven and place back on the stove over medium-high heat. Add the butter to melt. Using a spoon, baste the steak with the melted butter for 2 minutes. Remove the skillet from the heat, cover with aluminum foil, and let the steak rest for 5 minutes.

5. While the steak rests, place the watermelon, cotija cheese, and mint in a medium bowl and toss to combine. Drizzle with the vinaigrette and toss to combine.

6. Slice the steak against the grain into strips and place on top of the salad. Serve while the steak is warm.

INGREDIENT TIP: Cotija cheese versus queso fresco: What's the difference? They're both crumbly, soft, and white. Both are common cheeses in Mexican cooking. Queso fresco has a slightly salty, tangy flavor and is similar to farmer's cheese. Cotija cheese has a saltier, spongier consistency and works better in this salad because of the salty and sweet pairing of the cheese with the watermelon.

PER SERVING

Calories: 858; Fat: 76g; Sodium: 746mg; Carbohydrates: 17g; Protein: 32g; Fiber: 3g

FAJITA CHICKEN AND PEPPER SALAD

SERVES 3 OR 4

PREP TIME: 30 MINUTES / FINISH TIME: 5 MINUTES / TOTAL TIME: 35 MINUTES

GLUTEN-FREE, NUT-FREE

Fajitas are one of my favorite dishes to order in Mexican restaurants. Half of the reason is the hot sizzling sound the massive plate of grilled meat and peppers makes when it's served. The other reason is because fajitas are so fun to assemble. In Spanish, *faja* means strip or belt, which is indicative of the strips of meat and vegetables typically served. To turn this into a satisfying, flavorful salad, I like to serve it over wild rice. I don't blame you if this becomes your new favorite grain bowl.

1 cup wild rice **B**

1 pound chicken breast **P**

Salt

Freshly ground black pepper

½ teaspoon ground cumin

½ teaspoon paprika

2 bell peppers (red, yellow, green, or a mix) **V**

1 large onion **B**

4 tablespoons canola or vegetable oil, divided

½ teaspoon sugar

6 tablespoons Roasted Poblano Crema (page 161)

1 cup loosely packed fresh cilantro leaves, coarsely chopped **T**

1. Cook the wild rice according to the instructions on page 14.

2. While the rice cooks, place the chicken strips on a layer of plastic wrap and cover with a second layer of plastic wrap. With a meat tenderizer, pound the chicken to tenderize it. Season the chicken generously with salt and pepper, and with the cumin and paprika.

3. Cut the tenderized chicken and the bell peppers into long strips. Halve the onion crosswise and cut into strips.

4. Heat 2 tablespoons of oil in a large skillet over high heat. When the oil is hot, add the chicken strips in a single layer. Sear on both sides, about 2 minutes per side. Cover the skillet, reduce the heat to medium-high, and continue cooking the chicken for about 10 minutes. Uncover the skillet, increase the heat to high, and cook the chicken for about 1 minute more. Transfer to a plate.

5. Add the remaining 2 tablespoons of oil to the skillet over medium-high heat. When the oil is hot, add the bell peppers and onions. Sprinkle the vegetables with the sugar to help speed up the caramelization. Cook, stirring occasionally, for about 15 minutes, or until the peppers are very soft. Return the chicken the skillet and stir to combine. Remove the skillet from the heat.

6. Divide the rice among three or four plates. Top with the fajita mixture, drizzle with the crema, and garnish with the cilantro. Serve warm.

INGREDIENT TIP: Bell peppers—red, yellow, orange, green: Which do I choose? The difference in color comes from the time of harvest and how ripe the peppers are. Green peppers are the least ripe, and are therefore typically the cheapest. Each color of bell pepper has its own unique health benefits. Red bell peppers contain lycopene, and orange bell peppers have beta-carotene. For the best flavor (and most impressive presentation), use as many different types of bell peppers as possible.

PER SERVING

Calories: 650; Fat: 29g; Sodium: 252mg; Carbohydrates: 56g; Protein: 45g; Fiber: 6g

ARUGULA, BEAN, CORN, AND CHIMICHURRI STEAK SALAD

SERVES 2

PREP TIME: 30 MINUTES / FINISH TIME: 5 MINUTES / TOTAL TIME: 35 MINUTES

NUT-FREE

A healthy, Argentine-inspired salad with chimichurri flank steak, corn, beans, and arugula. This salad is an ode to my college, whose mascot is the Gaucho. *Olé olé olé!*

2 tablespoons extra-virgin olive oil

1 garlic clove, minced

1 fresh rosemary sprig or 1 teaspoon dried rosemary

2 (4-ounce) flank steaks P

Salt

Freshly ground black pepper

1 tablespoon unsalted butter

4 cups baby arugula B

1 cup pinto beans, drained and rinsed B

1 cup drained canned sweet corn V

¼ cup Chimichurri Vinaigrette, plus additional for garnish (page 164)

1. Preheat the oven to 375°F.

2. In a resealable bag, combine the olive oil, garlic, rosemary, and flank steak. Seal the bag and massage the meat to coat it in the marinade. Set aside to marinate for 15 minutes.

3. Remove the steak from the marinade (discarding the liquid) and season generously on both sides with salt and pepper. Place an oven-safe medium skillet over high heat. When the pan is very hot, add the steak and sear on both sides, about 2 minutes per side. Transfer the skillet to the oven and continue cooking the steak for 10 minutes.

4. Remove the skillet from the oven and place back on the stove over medium-high heat. Add the butter to melt. Using a spoon, baste the steak with the melted butter for 2 minutes. Remove the skillet from the heat, cover with aluminum foil, and let the steak rest for 5 minutes.

5. While the steak rests, toss the arugula, beans, and corn with the vinaigrette in a large bowl.

6. Slice the steak against the grain into strips. Divide the salad between two plates and top with the steak strips. Drizzle with more vinaigrette if desired. Serve while the steak is warm.

INGREDIENT TIP: Chimichurri is just as fun to eat as it is to write. It is a popular sauce used in Argentina, and pairs perfectly with red meat. Chimichurri is typically comprised of lots of fresh herbs, garlic, oil, and vinegar. A secret trick my sister-in-law'himichurri is typically comprised of lots of fresh herbs, garlic, oil, and vinegar. Chimichurri is typically comprised of lots of fresh

PER SERVING

Calories: 690; Fat: 48g; Sodium: 809mg; Carbohydrates: 37g; Protein: 34g; Fiber: 8g

TACO SALAD

SERVES 4

PREP TIME: 30 MINUTES / FINISH TIME: 5 MINUTES / TOTAL TIME: 35 MINUTES

GLUTEN-FREE, NUT-FREE

Don't wait until Tuesday to eat tacos. And you don't have to eat them with a tortilla. Taco salads have been on restaurant menus for decades. And while those huge, crisp tortilla bowls they are often served in are delicious, they are definitely not light in calories. This hearty and satisfying deconstructed taco salad bowl gives you all the great flavors and ingredients of a taco salad, but you won't be consuming all your daily calories in a single meal.

1 tablespoon canola oil
1 pound ground beef **P**
1½ teaspoons taco seasoning
8 cups shredded romaine lettuce **B**
2 cups cherry tomatoes, halved **V**
1 cup shredded Cheddar cheese **T**
2 cups tortilla chips, roughly crumbled
¾ cup pitted black olives, sliced into rings (optional) **B**
½ cup Roasted Poblano Crema (page 161)

1. Heat the oil in a large skillet over medium-high heat. Add the ground beef, mix in the taco seasoning, and cook, breaking the meat up with a wooden spoon, until fully browned and cooked through, about 6 minutes.

2. Arrange the salad on each of four plates. Begin with the romaine lettuce, then add the ground beef, tomatoes, and cheese, and top with the tortilla chips. Add the sliced black olives (if using). Drizzle with the poblano crema and serve warm.

INGREDIENT TIP: Ground beef is an easy way to sneak a ton of flavor and protein into your diet. Nowadays you can get super-lean ground beef (99 percent lean). A reasonable percentage that is healthy but still satisfying is 93 percent lean—you still get necessary fats without compromising on flavor or your waist size. If I want to really splurge, I love getting the 80 percent lean ground beef.

INGREDIENT TIP: Taco seasoning is generally a blend of cumin, paprika, onion powder, garlic powder, red pepper flakes, dried oregano, salt, and pepper.

PER SERVING

Calories: 660; Fat: 46g; Sodium: 699mg; Carbohydrates: 35g; Protein: 28g; Fiber: 3g

TEQUILA ORANGE CHICKEN AND QUINOA SALAD

SERVES 3

PREP TIME: 30 MINUTES / FINISH TIME: 5 MINUTES / TOTAL TIME: 35 MINUTES

GLUTEN-FREE, NUT-FREE

Have leftover tequila from last night's shenanigans? Get your meat (slightly) drunk! Marinating meat in alcohol may sound strange, but it helps tenderize the proteins and adds sugar, which helps with the browning process. Just be careful with the quantity of alcohol added, as well as with the marinating time (see Technique tip). This healthy grain salad bowl gets just the right amount of kick from tequila.

1 cup quinoa B
2 large oranges V
¼ cup silver tequila
½ teaspoon ground cumin
Salt
Freshly ground black pepper
¼ teaspoon chili powder or cayenne pepper (optional)
¾ pound chicken breast, cut into bite-size pieces P
1 tablespoon canola oil
6 tablespoons Tajín-Citrus Vinaigrette (page 149)
1 cup crumbled queso fresco T

1. Cook the quinoa according to the instructions on page 13. Fluff the cooked quinoa with a fork.

2. While the quinoa cooks, peel 1 orange and cut it into wedges. Cut the second orange in half. Juice one half into a medium bowl and peel the second half and cut it into wedges.

3. Add the tequila to the bowl with the orange juice along with the cumin, salt, pepper, and chili powder (if using) and stir to combine. Add the chicken and toss to coat it in the marinade. Marinate in the refrigerator for no more than 15 minutes.

4. Heat the canola oil in a medium skillet over medium-high heat. When the oil is hot, remove the chicken from the marinade and add to the skillet. Cook the chicken, stirring occasionally, until cooked through, about 10 minutes.

5. Divide the quinoa between three bowls. Top with the cooked chicken and the orange wedges. Drizzle the salads with the vinaigrette and garnish with the queso fresco. Serve warm.

TECHNIQUE TIP: Be careful with the quantity of alcohol used to tenderize the meat, as well as with the length of marinating time. Too much alcohol or too long marinating can "burn" through the meat, making it very tough.

PER SERVING

Calories: 662; Fat: 32g; Sodium: 215mg; Carbohydrates: 52g; Protein: 37g; Fiber: 7g

MEXICAN BROCCOLI SLAW
WITH SHRIMP

SERVES 3 OR 4

PREP TIME: 30 MINUTES / FINISH TIME: 5 MINUTES / TOTAL TIME: 35 MINUTES

GLUTEN-FREE, NUT-FREE, DAIRY-FREE

When most people think of slaw, they think of cabbage. But many other vegetables can be made into a slaw, including Brussels sprouts (shave or shred them) and broccoli. Broccoli slaw is made from the vegetable's stalk, which is separated from the florets and then shredded. It's crunchy, sweet, and a great way to add extra texture, flavor, and nutrition to a traditional slaw.

3 cups broccoli slaw **B**

2 cups shredded carrots **V**

1 cup shredded purple cabbage **V**

6 tablespoons Tajín-Citrus Vinaigrette (page 149)

½ tablespoon canola oil

1 pound shrimp, peeled and deveined **P**

Salt

Freshly ground black pepper

1 cup pepitas **T**

1. Combine the broccoli slaw, carrots, and purple cabbage in a large bowl. Drizzle with the vinaigrette and toss to combine.

2. Heat the oil in a large skillet over medium-high heat. Add the shrimp and season with salt and pepper. Cook until pink on both sides and cooked through, about 2 minutes per side.

3. In a small skillet, toast the pepitas according to the instructions on page 15.

4. Divide the broccoli slaw mixture among three or four bowls. Top with the shrimp and garnish with the pepitas. Serve at room temperature.

INGREDIENT TIP: Pepitas are pumpkin seeds. They are mild in flavor and add a wonderful crunchy texture to salads such as this slaw. Whenever you roast pumpkins, don't throw away the seeds. Toast them and keep on hand for when you need a snack or a great garnish for your salad.

PER SERVING

Calories: 587; Fat: 38g; Sodium: 495mg; Carbohydrates: 21g; Protein: 42g; Fiber: 6g

MANGO SHRIMP AND RICE CEVICHE SALAD

SERVES 3 OR 4

PREP TIME: 30 MINUTES / FINISH TIME: 5 MINUTES / TOTAL TIME: 35 MINUTES

GLUTEN-FREE, NUT-FREE, DAIRY-FREE

Ceviche is one of my absolute favorite things ever. It's a cold seafood salad. The raw seafood is "cooked" by the natural acid in citrus fruit, which flavors the seafood and tenderizes it at the same time. This ceviche served with wild rice, avocado, fresh sweet mango, and tangy lime juice is a flavor-packed and healthy salad.

Juice of 2 limes

6 tablespoons Honey-Orange Vinaigrette (page 151)

1½ pounds shrimp, peeled and deveined P

1 cup wild rice B

1 large, ripe mango, diced V

1 avocado, sliced B

Salt

Freshly ground black pepper

½ cup loosely packed fresh cilantro leaves, finely chopped T

1. In a large bowl, whisk together the lime juice and vinaigrette. Add the shrimp and toss to coat. Refrigerate for 30 minutes.

2. Cook the wild rice according to the instructions on page 14. Fluff the cooked rice with a fork.

3. Divide the rice among three or four bowls. Top with the shrimp, avocado, and mango. Season with salt and pepper and garnish with the cilantro. Serve cold.

OPTIONAL TIP: If you're feeling spicy, add 1 minced jalapeño, serrano, or habanero chile. Ceviche is often served with tortilla chips. For a nice crunch in contrast to the softer textures in the salad, loosely crumble some tortillas chips and use as a garnish.

PER SERVING

Calories: 659; Fat: 22g; Sodium: 409mg; Carbohydrates: 61g; Protein: 55g; Fiber: 5g

STRAWBERRY, CORN, AND BLACK BEAN SALAD

SERVES 2 OR 3

PREP TIME: 10 MINUTES / FINISH TIME: 5 MINUTES / TOTAL TIME: 15 MINUTES

VEGETARIAN, GLUTEN-FREE

Trust me on the strawberries-and-bean combination—it may sound weird, but it's magical.

1 (15-ounce) can black beans, drained and rinsed B
1 cup drained canned sweet corn V
2 cups ripe strawberries V
½ cup pepitas or sunflower seeds T
½ cup crumbled cotija cheese B
¼ cup Honey-Orange Vinaigrette (page 151)
Salt
Freshly ground black pepper

1. Place the beans and corn in a medium bowl.

2. Cut the strawberries following the Technique tip or cut into quarters.

3. Add the strawberries, pepitas, and cotija cheese to the bowl with the beans and corn. Drizzle with the vinaigrette and toss to combine. Season with salt and pepper.

4. Divide the salad between two or three bowls. Serve cold.

TECHNIQUE TIP: To make the strawberries look extra fancy, take a thin skewer and poke through the top center of the fruit. This will create a "tunnel" to remove the green tops. Cut the strawberries in half lengthwise, then cut crosswise into thin slices. They will look U-shaped.

PER SERVING
Calories: 650; Fat: 33g; Sodium: 1,444mg; Carbohydrates: 71g; Protein: 26g; Fiber: 23g

MEXICAN PASTA SALAD

SERVES 3 OR 4
PREP TIME: 20 MINUTES / FINISH TIME: 5 MINUTES / TOTAL TIME: 25 MINUTES
VEGETARIAN

Pasta is a neutral canvas for flavors from all around the world. It can really go in any direction. When in doubt, go pasta. This Mexican salad combines pasta, kidney beans, scallions, pepitas, and cotija cheese for a filling meal. The avocado-yogurt dressing adds creamy texture and tang to balance out the dish and enhance the flavors of the other ingredients.

8 ounces rotini pasta **B**
1 (15-ounce) can kidney beans, drained and rinsed **P**
4 scallions, green parts only, thinly sliced
½ cup pepitas or sunflower seeds **T**
¾ cup crumbled cotija cheese **B**
6 tablespoons Avocado-Yogurt Dressing (page 157)
Salt
Freshly ground black pepper

MAKE-AHEAD TIP: This is a perfect meal-prep-friendly dish. The undressed pasta salad can be made entirely ahead of time and refrigerated for up to 2 days. When you're ready to eat, just toss it with the dressing and dinner is served.

PER SERVING
Calories: 624; Fat: 19g; Sodium: 942mg; Carbohydrates: 91g; Protein: 28g; Fiber: 15g

1. Cook the rotini according to the package instructions or the instructions according to Step 1 on page 48. Drain the pasta and run it under cold water. Place in a medium bowl.

2. Add the beans, scallion greens, pepitas, cotija, and dressing. Season with salt and pepper and toss to combine.

3. Divide the salad between three or four bowls. Serve at room temperature.

JICAMA, STRAWBERRY, AND CHICKEN SALAD

SERVES 3

PREP TIME: 20 MINUTES / FINISH TIME: 5 MINUTES / TOTAL TIME: 25 MINUTES

GLUTEN-FREE, NUT-FREE

Jicama is sometimes referred to as a Mexican potato because it is used ubiquitously in Mexican cuisine, but flavor-wise it couldn't be more different from a potato. Jicama is a root vegetable that's often found in food preparations throughout Latin America. It is crispy and juicy like a pear, with a slightly sweet taste. It is a great vehicle for both sweet and savory salads, including this one.

1 cup quinoa **B**

½ pound chicken breast **P**

Salt

Freshly ground black pepper

2 tablespoons grapeseed, vegetable, or canola oil

1 medium jicama, cut into thin strips (about 2 to 2½ cups) **B**

2 cups strawberries, sliced **V**

2 large radishes, thinly sliced **T**

6 tablespoons Avocado-Yogurt Dressing (page 157)

1. Cook the quinoa according to the instructions on page 13. Fluff the cooked quinoa with a fork.

2. Tenderize and cook the chicken according to the instructions on page 15. Use salt and pepper to season the chicken and the oil to cook it. Slice the cooked chicken into bite-size pieces.

3. Divide the quinoa and chicken between three bowls. Top with the jicama, strawberries, and radishes. Drizzle the salads with the dressing. Serve warm.

PER SERVING

Calories: 550; Fat: 19g; Sodium: 134mg; Carbohydrates: 67g; Protein: 30g; Fiber: 19g

MEXICAN BEAN SALAD

SERVES 3 OR 4

PREP TIME: 10 MINUTES / FINISH TIME: 5 MINUTES / TOTAL TIME: 15 MINUTES

VEGAN, GLUTEN-FREE, NUT-FREE, DAIRY-FREE

This salad is dedicated to my roommate, Sydney, who swears that eating beans means you will live forever. It's working out well for her so far. This trio of beans marinated with a tangy vinaigrette and topped with creamy avocado and spicy radishes will help her and us to test that theory. Long live the bean!

½ (15-ounce) can kidney beans, drained and rinsed **B**

½ (15-ounce) can pinto beans, drained and rinsed **B**

½ (15-ounce) can black beans, drained and rinsed **B**

2 avocados, diced **T**

2 large radishes, thinly sliced **V**

Salt

Freshly ground black pepper

6 tablespoons Tajín-Citrus Vinaigrette (page 149)

In a large bowl, combine the kidney beans, pinto beans, black beans, avocados, and radishes. Season with salt and pepper. Add the vinaigrette and gently toss to combine. Divide among three or four plates and serve at room temperature.

MAKE-AHEAD TIP: Not only can this salad be made ahead, it's recommended. The longer the beans marinate in the vinaigrette, the better the flavors fuse.

PER SERVING

Calories: 687; Fat: 48g; Sodium: 298mg; Carbohydrates: 55g; Protein: 17g; Fiber: 24g

KIDNEY BEAN, TOMATO, AND SOFT-BOILED EGG SALAD

SERVES 2

PREP TIME: 10 MINUTES / FINISH TIME: 5 MINUTES / TOTAL TIME: 15 MINUTES

VEGETARIAN, GLUTEN-FREE, NUT-FREE, DAIRY-FREE

Topping salads—or just about any dish—with eggs is a great way to add another source of protein. Each type of preparation—soft-boiled, hard-boiled, or poached—offers its own unique texture to the dish. Eggs are also quick to make, so the protein you want for your salad is only minutes away. They are particularly great on top of Mexican dishes, the velvety yolk providing a nice counterbalance to the heat of the spices.

3 large eggs **P**
1 (15-ounce) can kidney beans, drained and rinsed **B**
2 cups cherry tomatoes, halved **V**
2 large radishes, thinly sliced **T**
6 tablespoons Tajín-Citrus Vinaigrette (page 149)
Salt
Freshly ground black pepper
1 cup tortilla strips **B**

1. Soft-boil the eggs according to the instructions on page 14. Chill and peel.

2. In a large bowl, combine the beans, tomatoes, and radishes. Drizzle with the vinaigrette and gently toss to combine. Season with salt and pepper.

3. Divide the salad among two bowls. Quarter the soft-boiled eggs lengthwise and place on top of each salad. Season with salt and pepper and garnish with the tortilla strips. Serve at room temperature.

OPTIONAL TIP: Mix in cooked farro or wild rice for additional fiber and an even more filling salad.

PER SERVING

Calories: 750; Fat: 40g; Sodium: 1,050mg; Carbohydrates: 77g; Protein: 28g; Fiber: 18g

BLACK BEAN AND CORN FRITTER SALAD

SERVES 3

PREP TIME: 10 MINUTES / FINISH TIME: 5 MINUTES / TOTAL TIME: 15 MINUTES

VEGETARIAN, NUT-FREE, DAIRY-FREE

A fritter is a lightly fried mix of ingredients. It can be sweet, savory, vegetarian, or for the meat lover. Fritters are wonderful to include on your dinner salad because they elevate otherwise run-of-the-mill ingredients into something extra flavorful, crispy, and comforting. Leftover beans and vegetables can be transformed into little nuggets of gold.

1 (15-ounce) can black beans, drained and rinsed [P]

1 cup drained canned sweet corn [B]

1 large egg, beaten

¼ cup all-purpose flour, plus more if needed

Pinch ground cumin

Pinch paprika

Salt

Freshly ground black pepper

Grapeseed or other neutral oil, for frying

5 or 6 cups mixed greens [B]

¼ cup Tajín-Citrus Vinaigrette (page 149)

2 cups cherry tomatoes, halved [V]

2 large radishes, thinly sliced [T]

1. Lightly mash the black beans, and combine with the corn in a medium bowl. Add the egg, flour, cumin, paprika, salt, and pepper. Stir to combine. The mixture should be moist and hold together when formed into patties. If it is too wet, mix in a little more flour. Form the mixture into small patties.

2. Heat a thin layer of oil in a large skillet over medium-high heat. When the oil is hot, add the patties and pan-fry until golden brown on one side, about 3 minutes. Flip and cook until golden brown on the other side, about 2 minutes more. Transfer the patties to a paper towel-lined plate and season with the salt and pepper.

3. In a large bowl, toss the mixed greens with the vinaigrette.

4. Divide the salad among three bowls. Top with the fritters, tomatoes, and radishes. Serve while the fritters are still warm.

OPTIONAL TIP: Add fresh cilantro leaves to the fritters for a bright, fresh, and earthy component. If you're feeling ambitious, you can also transform them into veggie burgers—just make bigger patties and serve them on buns topped with the dressed greens, tomatoes, and radishes.

PER SERVING

Calories: 671; Fat: 28g; Sodium: 352mg; Carbohydrates: 85g; Protein: 27g; Fiber: 23g

STRAWBERRY FIELDS CHICKEN SALAD   *page 141*

CHAPTER 7

AMERICAN-INSPIRED SALADS

This chapter includes some of my favorite American-inspired dinner salads. For a taste of the South in your mouth, try the Fried Chicken and Corn Bread Crouton Salad (page 132). Or fly across the country to California and reimagine the Cobb salad, a Hollywood staple made famous at the Brown Derby restaurant, with my Shrimp Cobb Salad (page 139) or Southwestern Cobb Salad (page 140). Or for Thanksgiving flavors without the tryptophan-induced food coma, try my Cranberry, Pumpkin, and Pecan Salad (page 130).

DECONSTRUCTED AVOCADO TOAST SALAD

SERVES 1

PREP TIME: 10 MINUTES / FINISH TIME: 5 MINUTES / TOTAL TIME: 15 MINUTES

NUT-FREE, DAIRY-FREE

It doesn't get more trendy than avocado toast—it is the quintessential brunch item on many a restaurant menu. These toasts have exploded across the country, and it's easy to see why: The creamy avocado is delicious and loaded with healthy fats. This deconstructed avocado toast salad is an ode to the breakfast version I eat at least twice a week.

2 large eggs B
1 cup microgreens B
2 tablespoons Lemon Vinaigrette (page 146)
2 oz. smoked salmon lox P
½ medium avocado, thinly sliced V
½ cup croutons T

1. Poach the eggs according to the instructions on page 14. Remove them from the liquid and pat dry with a paper towel.

2. Place the microgreens on a salad plate and toss with the vinaigrette.

3. Place the lox, avocado, and croutons on the microgreens and top with the poached eggs.

SUBSTITUTION TIP: Use bacon instead of smoked salmon lox.

TECHNIQUE TIP: Making your own croutons is very easy, and they are so much more flavorful than most prepackaged varieties. Simply cube your preferred bread and place in a hot skillet with some oil or melted butter. Toast until golden brown on all sides. Transfer to a paper towel–lined plate and season with salt and freshly ground black pepper.

PER SERVING

Calories: 711; Fat: 58g; Sodium: 1,526mg; Carbohydrates: 23g; Protein: 28g; Fiber: 9g

AVOCADO, SHRIMP, AND CORN SALAD

SERVES 1

PREP TIME: 5 MINUTES / FINISH TIME: 5 MINUTES / TOTAL TIME: 10 MINUTES

GLUTEN-FREE, NUT-FREE, DAIRY-FREE

ASC—avocado, shrimp, and corn. It's just as iconic as the BLT in my book. Easy, fast, and loaded with healthy fats and starches.

2½ cups torn romaine lettuce **B**
6 ounces cooked shrimp **P**
½ cup drained canned sweet corn **V**
½ medium avocado, thinly sliced **B**
2 tablespoons bacon bits **T**
2 tablespoons Lemon Vinaigrette (page 146)

1. Combine the romaine, shrimp, corn, avocado, and bacon bits in a large salad bowl.
2. Drizzle the salad with the vinaigrette and toss to combine. Serve cold.

OPTIONAL TIP: Store-bought precooked shrimp works perfectly, but raw shrimp can be used, too. Shrimp is very quick to cook, and making it from scratch opens the door for extra flavor. Heat a small skillet with 1 tablespoon of olive oil. Add 1 small clove of minced garlic and cook for about 30 seconds, or until aromatic. Add the shelled and deveined shrimp and cook for 2 to 4 minutes, or until pink and cooked through.

PER SERVING

Calories: 727; Fat: 50g; Sodium: 678mg; Carbohydrates: 28g; Protein: 47g; Fiber: 9g

BACON, ROASTED BRUSSELS SPROUT, POMEGRANATE, AND FETA SALAD

SERVES 1

PREP TIME: 40 MINUTES / FINISH TIME: 5 MINUTES / TOTAL TIME: 45 MINUTES

GLUTEN-FREE, NUT-FREE

I remember exactly where I was when I first had bacon with Brussels sprouts— it was truly a legendary day. I loved this salad before I discovered bacon, and I've been bedazzling it with bacon since then to take it to the next level. Bacon is fatty and rich, Brussels sprouts have a filling bite, pomegranate seeds are sweet and refreshing, and feta cheese is savory and salty. It all works together to make my mouth happy!

2 cups small Brussels sprouts **B**
3 ounces bacon **P**
½ cup pomegranate seeds **V**
½ cup crumbled feta cheese
   (preferably sheep's milk) **T**

1. Preheat the oven to 375°F.

2. Roast the Brussels sprouts according to the instructions on page 12.

3. While the Brussels sprouts roast, fry the bacon in a skillet over medium heat for 8 to 10 minutes, or until cooked through. Transfer to a paper towel-lined plate and pat any excess fat from the bacon with a paper towel. Cut the bacon into bite-size pieces.

4. Place the roasted Brussels sprouts on a plate. Top with the bacon, pomegranate seeds, and feta cheese. Serve warm.

OPTIONAL TIP: To cut down the prep time by about half, shave the Brussels sprouts instead of roasting them. To do this, trim the Brussels sprouts and, with a knife or a mandoline, slice into thin strips (as thin as possible). Sauté the sprouts in the residual bacon fat and season with salt and pepper. Transfer to a plate and top with the bacon, pomegranate seeds, and feta cheese.

PER SERVING
Calories: 565; Fat: 43g; Sodium: 1,027mg; Carbohydrates: 19g; Protein: 23g; Fiber: 8g

BARBECUE CHICKEN PIZZA SALAD

SERVES 2 OR 3

PREP TIME: 15 MINUTES / FINISH TIME: 5 MINUTES / TOTAL TIME: 20 MINUTES

GLUTEN-FREE, NUT-FREE

Whoever invented the combination of chicken, barbecue sauce, red onions, and cheese deserves a medal. My former roommate Frank was obsessed with barbecue sauce. When he moved in, he brought over 20 bottles of craft sauces. This salad is dedicated to you, Frank. Thanks for the barbecue sauce tasting and thanks for inspiring this meal.

1 tablespoon canola oil

2 (6-ounce) chicken thighs, cut into bite-size pieces P

⅓ cup barbecue sauce

4 cups torn romaine lettuce B

2 scallions, green parts only, thinly sliced

2 tablespoons pickled red onion (page 13) or diced red onion B

⅓ cup shredded white Cheddar cheese T

1. Heat the oil in a large skillet over medium-high heat. When hot, add the chicken and cook, stirring occasionally, until cooked through, about 8 minutes.

2. Transfer the chicken to a medium bowl and toss with the barbecue sauce.

3. Divide the romaine between two or three plates. Top with the chicken, scallions, pickled red onion, and cheese. Serve while the chicken is still warm.

SHORTCUT TIP: One of my favorite easy, go-to meals is store-bought whole rotisserie chicken. For this salad, shred the meat and toss it in the barbecue sauce. An already easy meal just got even easier.

PER SERVING

Calories: 584; Fat: 39g; Sodium: 720mg; Carbohydrates: 21g; Protein: 36g; Fiber: 3g

BLTE PANZANELLA SALAD

SERVES 2

PREP TIME: 20 MINUTES / FINISH TIME: 5 MINUTES / TOTAL TIME: 25 MINUTES

NUT-FREE, DAIRY-FREE

Bread salads are totally a thing, right? Panzanella is a traditional Italian salad made with soaked stale bread and fresh summer tomatoes. I'm taking it a step further and including the flavors of that American classic, the bacon, lettuce, and tomato sandwich. And why not take it yet one step further and throw an egg on top?

4 bacon strips **P**

4 slices bread (any kind works), cubed **T**

Salt

Freshly ground black pepper

2 large eggs **B**

4 or 5 cups torn romaine lettuce **B**

1½ cups cherry tomatoes, halved **V**

¼ cup Honey-Mustard Vinaigrette (page 150)

1. Place a medium skillet over medium heat and fry the bacon until cooked through, 8 to 10 minutes. Leaving the rendered fat in the skillet, transfer the bacon to a paper towel-lined plate and pat any excess fat from the bacon with a paper towel. Cut the bacon into bite-size pieces.

2. Toast the bread cubes in the bacon fat until the bread turns into crispy croutons, about 5 minutes. Transfer to a paper towel-lined plate and season with salt and pepper.

3. Poach the eggs according to the instructions on page 14. Remove them from the liquid and gently pat dry with a paper towel.

4. Divide the romaine between two plates. Top with the tomatoes, bacon, and croutons. Add a poached egg to each salad and drizzle with the vinaigrette. Serve while the eggs are still warm.

PER SERVING

Calories: 562; Fat: 48g; Sodium: 615mg; Carbohydrates: 17g; Protein: 17g; Fiber: 3g

BUTTERNUT SQUASH, SUNFLOWER SEED, AND SHAVED PARMESAN SALAD

SERVES 2

PREP TIME: 10 MINUTES / FINISH TIME: 5 MINUTES / TOTAL TIME: 15 MINUTES

VEGETARIAN

If it's starting to get chilly outside and you're itching to pull out your sweater, pull out this recipe while you're at it. This fall salad will warm your heart.

1 medium butternut squash, peeled, seeded, and cut into cubes B
1 cup sunflower seeds, toasted T
¼ cup Lemon-Tahini Dressing (page 158)
Salt
Freshly ground black pepper
½ cup shaved high-quality Parmesan cheese B

1. Preheat the oven to 350°F.

2. Roast the butternut squash according to the instructions on page 12.

3. Place the sunflower seeds on a baking sheet and toast in the oven for about 5 minutes.

4. Cut the roasted butternut squash into bite-size pieces and place in a medium bowl along with the toasted sunflower seeds. Add the dressing and toss to combine. Season with salt and pepper.

5. Divide the salad between two plates and garnish with the Parmesan. Serve warm.

INGREDIENT TIP: Butternut squash is often referred to as winter squash in the United States, but it is actually picked only in the fall.

SUBSTITUTION TIP: Try this salad with roasted sugar pumpkin or sweet potatoes.

PER SERVING

Calories: 520; Fat: 34g; Sodium: 404mg; Carbohydrates: 44g; Protein: 21g; Fiber: 10g

CRANBERRY, PUMPKIN, AND PECAN SALAD

SERVES 3 OR 4

PREP TIME: 1 HOUR 15 MINUTES / FINISH TIME: 5 MINUTES / TOTAL TIME: 1 HOUR 20 MINUTES

VEGAN, GLUTEN-FREE, DAIRY-FREE

It doesn't need to be Thanksgiving to enjoy these classic American flavors. After all, aren't the side dishes the best part of the meal? These warm fall flavors make for a hearty and healthy dinner salad. Smooth, creamy pumpkin, crunchy pecans, and tangy cranberries combine to create the perfect bite.

2 small sugar pumpkins **V**
⅓ cup dried cranberries **T**
½ cup pecans **B**
Brown sugar, for sprinkling
Salt
Freshly ground black pepper
5 cups frisée **B**
6 tablespoons Herb Vinaigrette
   (page 148)

1. Preheat the oven to 350°F.

2. Roast the pumpkins according to the instructions on page 13. Remove from the oven and leave the oven on.

3. Cut the roasted pumpkins in half. Scoop out the seeds into a small bowl, and scoop out the cooked pumpkin and place in a large bowl.

4. Wash the pumpkin seeds and dry them on a paper towel. Place on a baking sheet along with the pecans and cranberries. Sprinkle with brown sugar and toast in the oven for about 10 minutes.

5. Cut the pumpkin into bite-size pieces and season with salt and pepper. Add the frisée to the bowl along with the toasted pumpkin seeds, cranberries, and pecans. Drizzle with the vinaigrette and toss to combine.

6. Divide the salad between three or four plates. Serve warm.

SHORTCUT TIP: Buying precut pumpkin will save a lot of roasting time. Just toss it with extra-virgin olive oil, salt, and pepper and roast in the oven at 375°F for 20 minutes.

SUBSTITUTION TIP: Use butternut squash or sweet potatoes in place of the pumpkins.

PER SERVING

Calories: 390; Fat: 24g; Sodium: 78mg; Carbohydrates: 45g; Protein: 4g; Fiber: 5g

FARRO, HAZELNUT, AND BRUSSELS SPROUT SALAD

SERVES 2 OR 3

PREP TIME: 45 MINUTES / FINISH TIME: 5 MINUTES / TOTAL TIME: 50 MINUTES

VEGETARIAN

Hazelnuts are a wonderfully versatile nut. They are used in all kinds of confections—hazelnut cookies or pralines, anyone?—and they can even be made into soup. And, of course, hazelnut coffee is a perennial favorite. Here, hazelnuts paired with salty, earthy roasted Brussels sprouts is a divine combination. Factor in the nuttiness from the farro for an extra dimension of flavor, and you have the ultimate dinner salad.

1 cup farro **B**

1½ cups small Brussels sprouts, halved **V**

1 tablespoon extra-virgin olive oil

2 shallots, thinly sliced

½ cup hazelnuts **T**

½ cup shaved Parmesan cheese **B**

6 tablespoons Herb Vinaigrette (page 148)

1. Preheat the oven to 375°F.

2. Cook the farro according to the instructions on page 13. Fluff the cooked farro with a fork.

3. Roast the Brussels sprouts according to the instructions on page 12.

4. Heat the olive oil in a small skillet over medium-high heat. When hot, add the shallots and fry, stirring occasionally, until browned and slightly crispy, 3 to 4 minutes.

5. Divide the farro between two or three bowls. Add the roasted Brussels sprouts, hazelnuts, and fried shallots. Top with the shaved Parmesan and drizzle with the vinaigrette. Serve warm.

OPTIONAL TIP: To take this salad to the next level, caramelize the hazelnuts by tossing them with sugar and pan-"frying" in 1 tablespoon of unsalted butter. This adds a layer of caramelization and nuttiness to the dish that complements the farro and the sharpness of the Parmesan cheese.

PER SERVING

Calories: 410; Fat: 33g; Sodium: 204mg; Carbohydrates: 20g; Protein: 12g; Fiber: 5g

FRIED CHICKEN AND CORN BREAD CROUTON SALAD

SERVES 3

PREP TIME: 25 MINUTES / FINISH TIME: 5 MINUTES / TOTAL TIME: 30 MINUTES

NUT-FREE

If there are two foods that evoke the American South, fried chicken and corn bread are at the top of any list. Ask 10 Southerners their take on how to make fried chicken and corn bread and you're sure to get 10 different answers. While many have their own preferences, the common ingredient is love. Take a trip to the South by combining two Southern comfort foods and re-imagining them into a salad.

3 small chicken breasts
   (about 1 pound) **P**
¾ cup all-purpose flour
Salt
Freshly ground black pepper
1 large egg, beaten
1 cup buttermilk
Grapeseed, canola, or vegetable oil,
   for frying
3 slices day-old corn bread **T**
1 tablespoon unsalted butter
6 cups mixed greens **B**
1 cup drained canned sweet corn **B**
1 cup cherry tomatoes, halved **V**
6 tablespoons Buttermilk-Poppy
   Dressing (page 153)

1. Cut the chicken breasts in half crosswise. Place them on a layer of plastic wrap and cover with a second layer. Using a meat tenderizer, pound the chicken ½ inch to ¾ inch thick.

2. Place the flour on a large plate and season with the salt and pepper. Add the egg to a shallow bowl and the buttermilk to a separate shallow bowl.

3. Dredge each piece of chicken in the flour to coat, then dip in the egg. Dredge in the flour again, then dip in the buttermilk. For a third and final time, dredge in the flour to coat all over. Let the chicken sit in the buttermilk until it's ready to be fried.

4. Heat ¾ to 1 inch of oil in a large skillet over medium-high heat. When the oil is very hot, add the chicken and fry until golden brown on both sides, about 5 minutes per side. You may need to fry it in batches. Alternatively, use two large skillets to fry the chicken. Transfer the fried chicken to a paper towel-lined plate and season them with the salt and pepper.

5. While the chicken fries, cut the corn bread into cubes. Place a small skillet over high heat and melt the butter. Add the corn bread cubes and toast until they dry out and harden like croutons, about 5 minutes.

6. Divide the mixed greens, corn, tomatoes, and chicken among three bowls. Top with the corn bread croutons and drizzle with the dressing. Serve while the chicken is warm.

OPTIONAL TIP: If corn bread isn't on hand, use any stale bread instead to make the croutons.

PER SERVING
Calories: 679; Fat: 18g; Sodium: 896mg; Carbohydrates: 78g; Protein: 52g; Fiber: 5g

JERK CHICKEN SALAD

SERVES 3

PREP TIME: 35 MINUTES / FINISH TIME: 5 MINUTES / TOTAL TIME: 40 MINUTES

GLUTEN-FREE, NUT-FREE, DAIRY-FREE

Jerk, or *charqui* in Spanish (meaning "dried meat"), refers to a style of Jamaican cooking in which meat is marinated with a hot spice mixture. Jerk is probably the ultimate Jamaican dish—cooks there prepare all proteins—from chicken to goat to even fish—in this style. An ode to our Caribbean neighbors, this salad packs a ton of flavor and combines sweet with spicy for a full-on party in your mouth. If you can't take the heat, stay out of the kitchen.

¾ cup wild rice **B**

2 (4-ounce) chicken thighs, cut into bite-size pieces **P**

1 teaspoon jerk seasoning

Salt

Freshly ground black pepper

Canola oil, for frying

1 red bell pepper, cut into thin strips **V**

½ cup pineapple chunks **T**

1 mango, cubed **B**

6 tablespoons Honey-Mustard Vinaigrette (page 150)

1. Cook the wild rice according to the instructions on page 14.

2. Rub the chicken with the jerk seasoning and season with salt and pepper.

3. Heat a thin layer of oil in a medium skillet over medium-high heat. Add the chicken and fry until tender and cooked through, about 10 minutes. Transfer the chicken to a paper towel–lined plate.

4. Divide the wild rice between three bowls. Top with the chicken, bell pepper strips, pineapple, and mango. Drizzle with the vinaigrette. Serve warm.

MAKE-AHEAD TIP: Cut the chicken thighs into bite-size pieces a day in advance, rub with the jerk seasoning, and let sit overnight in the refrigerator in a resealable plastic bag. This will allow the jerk flavor to seep in more, and it will save you some prep time when you're ready to assemble the salad. You can even fry up a bigger batch of chicken and refrigerate it for up to 3 days, ready to be used for other dishes.

PER SERVING

Calories: 969; Fat: 53g; Sodium: 206mg; Carbohydrates: 96g; Protein: 34g; Fiber: 9g

KALE PESTO PASTA SALAD

SERVES 3

PREP TIME: 30 MINUTES / FINISH TIME: 5 MINUTES / TOTAL TIME: 35 MINUTES

VEGETARIAN

Traditional pesto is made with fresh basil, garlic, pine nuts, Parmesan, and extra-virgin olive oil. Over the years, it has been transformed with other ingredients; sometimes it's made with spinach, sometimes with mint, and sometimes even with cilantro or, yes, kale. The robust flavor of the walnuts here stands up to the sturdiness of the kale. Added to pasta, it makes for a downright great dinner salad.

3 cups fresh kale **V**

3 tablespoons walnuts **T**

½ cup grated Parmesan cheese, plus more for garnish **B**

⅓ cup extra-virgin olive oil, plus 2 tablespoons

1½ teaspoons freshly squeezed lemon juice

Salt

Freshly ground black pepper

6 ounces whole-wheat rotini or other pasta **B**

1. To make the pesto, place the kale in the bowl of a food processor or in a blender. Add the walnuts, ½ cup of Parmesan cheese, ⅓ cup of olive oil, the lemon juice, salt, and pepper and blend until smooth. Taste and adjust accordingly: If the pesto is too thick, add more lemon juice or oil. This yields a little less than 1 cup of pesto.

2. Cook the pasta according to the instructions in Step 1 on page 48. Reserve 1 tablespoon of the starchy pasta cooking water.

3. Heat the remaining 2 tablespoons of olive oil in a large skillet over medium heat. When hot, add the pesto and the reserved pasta water and heat for about 2 minutes, until they are incorporated. Add the pasta and stir to combine.

4. Divide the pasta salad between three bowls. Serve warm, garnished with freshly grated Parmesan cheese.

OPTIONAL TIP: To really take this salad to the next level, add steamed, roasted, or broiled broccoli for added flavor and nutrition.

PER SERVING

Calories: 804; Fat: 60g; Sodium: 385mg; Carbohydrates: 53g; Protein: 20g; Fiber: 7g

KALE, APPLE, AND PROSCIUTTO SALAD

SERVES 1

PREP TIME: 5 MINUTES / FINISH TIME: 5 MINUTES / TOTAL TIME: 10 MINUTES

GLUTEN-FREE, NUT-FREE

The combination of apple and prosciutto is almost as fundamental as peanut butter and jelly. The apple is sweet and tart, and the prosciutto is salty and fatty, and when they're combined, watch what happens! The kale, Parmesan, and honey-mustard vinaigrette are the cheerleaders of this salad, but the apple and prosciutto are definitely the rock stars.

3 cups chopped fresh kale B
3 tablespoons Honey-Mustard Vinaigrette (page 150)
1 medium apple V
4 slices prosciutto or Parma ham P
2 ounces Parmesan cheese T

1. In a large bowl, toss the kale in the vinaigrette to soften it. If you prefer, massage the kale as described on page 5.

2. Core the apple and thinly slice it.

3. Plate the dressed kale. Add the apple and prosciutto slices. Shave the Parmesan over each salad. Serve cold.

LEFTOVER TIP: If you bought way too much kale, a great way to use up leftovers is to make a pesto with it. See the Kale Pesto Pasta Salad recipe on the opposite page.

PER SERVING

Calories: 675; Fat: 41g; Sodium: 649mg; Carbohydrates: 46g; Protein: 40g; Fiber: 8g

QUINOA, ORANGE, GRAPEFRUIT, AND KIWI SALAD

SERVES 2

PREP TIME: 25 MINUTES / FINISH TIME: 5 MINUTES / TOTAL TIME: 30 MINUTES

VEGETARIAN, GLUTEN-FREE, NUT-FREE

Fruit salad makes for a wonderful, savory dinner. Serving it with quinoa, goat cheese, and pesto is a great way to sneak in your fruit serving for the day while also having a well-balanced, well-rounded meal. The orange, grapefruit, and kiwi are all amazing sources of vitamin C—the kiwi actually has more of it than the citrus.

⅔ cup quinoa **B**
1 orange, peeled and cut into large circles **V**
1 grapefruit, peeled and cut into wedges **V**
2 small kiwis, peeled and cut into circles **B**
4 ounces goat cheese, crumbled **T**
¼ cup Pesto Dressing (page 155)

1. Cook the quinoa according to the instructions on page 13. Fluff the cooked quinoa with a fork.

2. Divide the quinoa between two bowls. Top with the orange, grapefruit, kiwi, and goat cheese. Drizzle with the dressing. Serve cold.

INGREDIENT TIP: Kiwis are one of nature's best gifts. It's always astonishing to me to cut open a kiwi and see how vibrant and beautiful it is. Little-known fact: Kiwis originated in China and were initially called Chinese gooseberries. The name was changed to kiwi around 1960, reportedly as a result of anti-Communist sentiment.

PER SERVING

Calories: 730; Fat: 41g; Sodium: 215mg; Carbohydrates: 68g; Protein: 28g; Fiber: 10g

PUMPKIN-FARRO SALAD

SERVES 4
PREP TIME: 1 HOUR 10 MINUTES / FINISH TIME: 5 MINUTES / TOTAL TIME: 1 HOUR 15 MINUTES
VEGETARIAN

When most Americans think of pumpkin, they think of the large orange squash that we delightfully carve up for Halloween. They also think of pumpkin pie, but that and other dishes made with pumpkin aren't actually made from the Halloween kind of pumpkin, but from another variety called pie pumpkin, or sugar pumpkins. It is from them that we get our love of anything pumpkin.

2 small sugar pumpkins V
1 cup farro B
Salt
Freshly ground black pepper
¾ cup dried cranberries B
¾ cup walnuts T
¾ cup crumbled feta cheese P

1. Preheat the oven to 350°F.
2. Roast the pumpkins according to the instructions on page 13. Cut the roasted pumpkins in half and scoop out the flesh into a medium bowl. Reserve the seeds to toast at a later time, or discard.
3. Cook the farro according to the instructions on page 13. Fluff the cooked farro with a fork.
4. Cut the pumpkin into bite-size pieces and season with salt and pepper.
5. Divide the farro between four plates and top with the pumpkin. Garnish with the cranberries, walnuts, and feta cheese. Serve warm.

LEFTOVER TIP: Roasted pumpkin seeds will bedazzle your future salads. Pumpkin seeds are packed with protein and add a nice crunch when they're roasted. Place the seeds on a baking sheet and drizzle with a bit of extra-virgin olive oil. Season with salt and pepper and toss to combine. Roast the seeds for 5 to 8 minutes in a 350°F oven. For sweeter pumpkin seeds, roast them for 5 minutes with melted butter and brown sugar.

SUBSTITUTION TIP: If sugar pumpkins aren't available, try butternut squash or sweet potatoes instead.

PER SERVING
Calories: 352; Fat: 19g; Sodium: 357mg; Carbohydrates: 40g; Protein: 10g; Fiber: 4g

RICOTTA SALATA, BROCCOLI, PARMESAN, AND ALMOND SALAD

SERVES 2

PREP TIME: 25 MINUTES / FINISH TIME: 5 MINUTES / TOTAL TIME: 30 MINUTES

VEGETARIAN, GLUTEN-FREE

What's better than one cheese in a salad? Two cheeses, naturally. Ricotta salata is basically ricotta cheese that's been salted and aged. It's comparable in taste and texture to feta, but is milkier in flavor. It's an affordable cheese and, for me, a must-have ingredient for salads.

3 tablespoons extra-virgin olive oil, divided

2 shallots or 1 small onion, sliced into thin circles V

1 large garlic clove, minced

3 cups broccoli florets B

Salt

Freshly ground black pepper

¼ cup Lemon Vinaigrette (page 146)

½ cup ricotta salata P

¼ cup grated Parmesan cheese B

½ cup slivered almonds T

1. Heat 1 tablespoon of olive oil in a large skillet over medium-high heat. When hot, add the shallots and cook until soft and translucent, about 5 minutes. Add the garlic and cook until it is aromatic, 1 to 2 minutes. Transfer to a large bowl.

2. Heat the remaining 2 tablespoons of olive oil in the skillet over high heat. Add the broccoli florets, stir to cover with the oil, then cover the skillet. Steam the broccoli for about 5 minutes. Uncover and stir in the shallot mixture. Lightly season with salt and pepper and cook, stirring occasionally, for 5 minutes more.

3. Place the broccoli mixture in the large bowl and toss with the vinaigrette.

4. Divide the salad between two bowls. Crumble the ricotta salata over each and garnish with the Parmesan cheese and almonds. Serve warm.

OPTION TIP: You can prepare the broccoli for this salad multiple ways— steamed as in the recipe, but also roasted, pan-fried, or even uncooked.

PER SERVING

Calories: 705; Fat: 66g; Sodium: 225mg; Carbohydrates: 21g; Protein: 18g; Fiber: 8g

SHRIMP COBB SALAD

SERVES 1

PREP TIME: 15 MINUTES / FINISH TIME: 5 MINUTES / TOTAL TIME: 20 MINUTES

GLUTEN-FREE, NUT-FREE

To my mind, a Cobb salad is like eating the rainbow. Bright colors and vibrant flavors are its hallmark. There are no real rules when it comes to making a Cobb salad; you can customize it to your tastes and preferences. An old-school Cobb salad has eggs, avocados, tomatoes, grilled chicken, onions, bacon, blue cheese, and lettuce. This version changes things up by using shrimp, corn, and feta cheese—three ingredients that are well balanced when combined.

2 large eggs B
2 cups torn romaine lettuce B
4 ounces cooked shrimp, diced P
½ cup drained canned sweet corn V
⅓ cup crumbled feta cheese T
Salt
Freshly ground black pepper
2 tablespoons Avocado-Yogurt Dressing (page 157)

FREEZER TIP: Frozen precooked shrimp are one of the easiest ways to get protein in an affordable and realistic way. Simply thaw a few handfuls in a bowl of room-temperature water for about 20 minutes, and they're good to eat!

PER SERVING

Calories: 555; Fat: 29g; Sodium: 1,147mg; Carbohydrates: 26g; Protein: 5g; Fiber: 51g

1. Hard-boil the eggs according to the instructions on page 14. Chill, peel and dice the eggs.

2. Place the romaine on a plate. Add the shrimp in a long stripe across one side of the lettuce. Do the same with the eggs, corn, and crumbled feta so that the four ingredients are right in a row. Season the salad with salt and pepper and drizzle with the dressing. Serve at room temperature.

SOUTHWESTERN COBB SALAD

SERVES 2

PREP TIME: 10 MINUTES / FINISH TIME: 5 MINUTES / TOTAL TIME: 15 MINUTES

VEGETARIAN, NUT-FREE

This Tex-Mex-inspired Cobb salad is a great way to mix and match lots of bold flavors. Nevertheless, the chipotle dressing is the real star. It stands up to those bold flavors—creamy avocado, chewy beans, sharp Cheddar, and sweet corn— and transforms this salad from something pleasant to a total wow.

1 cup drained and rinsed black beans **P**
Salt
Freshly ground black pepper
4 cups torn romaine lettuce **B**
1 large avocado, diced **B**
⅔ cup drained canned sweet corn **V**
½ cup shredded Cheddar cheese **T**
½ cup Creamy Chipotle Dressing
    (page 156)

1. Place the beans in a small bowl and season them with salt and pepper.

2. Divide the romaine between two plates, then add a layer of avocado, black beans, corn, and Cheddar cheese. Drizzle with the dressing. Serve at room temperature.

LEFTOVER TIP: Leftover black beans and corn? They make a great base for fritters for tomorrow's dinner. See the recipe for Black Bean and Corn Fritter Salad on page 121.

PER SERVING

Calories: 553; Fat: 36g; Sodium: 416mg; Carbohydrates: 44g; Protein: 20g; Fiber: 16g

STRAWBERRY FIELDS CHICKEN SALAD

SERVES 1

PREP TIME: 20 MINUTES / FINISH TIME: 5 MINUTES / TOTAL TIME: 25 MINUTES

GLUTEN-FREE

To everyone who doesn't believe that fruit belongs in salads, try this out. The amazing combination of spinach, strawberries, chicken, and goat cheese is satisfying, well-balanced, and affordable.

1 small chicken breast
   (about 4 ounces) **P**
2 cups baby spinach **B**
2 tablespoons Buttermilk-Poppy Dressing
   (page 153)
1 cup sliced strawberries **V**
⅓ cup crumbled goat cheese **B**
¼ cup pecans **T**

1. Cook the chicken according to the instructions on page 15. Slice it into thin strips.

2. In a serving bowl or on a plate, toss the spinach with the dressing. Add the chicken, strawberries, goat cheese, and pecans. Serve warm.

TECHNIQUE TIP: Tenderizing chicken is especially important when you're using lean white meat like the breast. The best method is to brine the chicken, which involves soaking it in a brine of water, salt, and sugar for up to 2 days. A much faster technique is to pound the chicken with a meat tenderizer, which looks like a hammer with teeth. Or, if you don't have a meat tenderizer, an actual (clean) hammer works fine. Lay the chicken between two pieces of plastic wrap for easier cleanup.

PER SERVING

Calories: 579; Fat: 37g; Sodium: 317mg; Carbohydrates: 22g; Protein: 47g; Fiber: 6g

FLANK STEAK AND PEACH SALAD

SERVES 1

PREP TIME: 40 MINUTES / FINISH TIME: 5 MINUTES / TOTAL TIME: 45 MINUTES

GLUTEN-FREE, NUT-FREE

Steak and peaches is a fantastic combination of sweet and savory. Fresh peaches in season are hard to beat. Their wonderfully sweet juice also carries a slight acidic bite, making them the perfect accompaniment to the fattier flavor of the steak. All this salad is missing is a side shot of bourbon.

2 tablespoons extra-virgin olive oil
1 garlic clove, minced
1 rosemary sprig or 1 teaspoon dried rosemary
1 (4-ounce) flank steak P
1 peach, sliced V
½ teaspoon sugar
Salt
Freshly ground black pepper
1 tablespoon unsalted butter
2 cups baby spinach B
2 tablespoons Buttermilk-Poppy Dressing (page 153)
¼ cup crumbled blue cheese T

1. Preheat the oven to 375°F.

2. In a resealable bag, combine the olive oil, minced garlic, rosemary, and flank steak. Seal the bag and massage the meat to cover it in the marinade. Set aside to marinate for 15 minutes.

3. Place the peach slices in a small bowl and sprinkle them with the sugar.

4. Remove the steak from the marinade (discarding the liquid) and generously season on both sides with the salt and pepper. Place an oven-safe medium skillet over high heat. When it is very hot, add the steak and sear on both sides, about 2 minutes per side. Transfer the skillet to the oven and continue cooking the steak for 10 minutes.

5. Remove the skillet from the oven and place back on the stove over medium-high heat. Add the butter to melt. Using a spoon, baste the steak with the melted butter for 2 minutes. Remove the skillet from the heat, cover with aluminum foil, and let the steak rest for 5 minutes before slicing against the grain into strips.

6. Place the spinach on a plate and toss with the dressing. Add the steak strips and peach slices on top. Garnish the salad with the blue cheese. Serve warm.

INGREDIENT TIP: Macerating fruit is an easy, powerful trick in the kitchen anyone can master to make fruit much more flavorful. Simply add a bit of sugar onto the fruit, and let it sit for at least 15 minutes to let the fruit release its natural juices. This is a great hack, especially if your fruit isn't fully ripe.

PER SERVING

Calories: 780; Fat: 62g; Sodium: 876mg; Carbohydrates: 24g; Protein: 36g; Fiber: 4g

STEAK-AND-EGGS BREAKFAST SALAD

SERVES 1

PREP TIME: 45 MINUTES / FINISH TIME: 5 MINUTES / TOTAL TIME: 50 MINUTES

NUT-FREE

Breakfast salads are a new trend that I'm loving—they're a twist on a classic breakfast dish in the form of a revamped salad. You can find steak and eggs on most American brunch menus nowadays, and I'm all about it.

2 tablespoons extra-virgin olive oil

1 garlic clove, minced

1 fresh rosemary sprig or 1 teaspoon dried rosemary

1 (4-ounce) flank steak P

Salt

Freshly ground black pepper

2 eggs B

1 tablespoon unsalted butter

2 cups torn romaine lettuce B

2 tablespoons Honey-Mustard Vinaigrette (page 150)

⅔ cup cherry tomatoes, halved V

⅓ cup croutons T

1. Preheat the oven to 375°F.

2. In a resealable bag, combine the olive oil, minced garlic, rosemary, and flank steak. Seal the bag and massage the meat to cover it in the marinade. Set aside to marinate for 15 minutes.

3. Remove the steak from the marinade (discarding the liquid) and generously season on both sides with salt and pepper. Place an oven-safe medium skillet over high heat. When it is very hot, add the steak and sear on both sides, about 2 minutes per side. Transfer the skillet to the oven and continue cooking the steak for 10 minutes.

4. While the steak is in the oven, soft-boil the eggs according to the instructions on page 14. Carefully cut the eggs into quarters.

5. Remove the skillet from the oven and place back on the stove over medium-high heat. Add the butter to melt. Using a spoon, baste the steak with the melted butter for 2 minutes. Remove the skillet from the heat, cover with aluminum foil, and let the steak rest for 5 minutes before slicing against the grain into strips.

6. Place the romaine on a plate and toss with the vinaigrette. Add the tomatoes, steak strips, and eggs. Garnish the salad with the croutons. Serve warm.

INGREDIENT TIP: A little-known fact is that this breakfast dish is fit for an astronaut! Steak and eggs is the traditional preflight breakfast of NASA astronauts. It was first served to Alan Shepard before his flight on May 5, 1961.

PER SERVING

Calories: 891; Fat: 76g; Sodium: 535 g; Carbohydrates: 16g; Protein: 39g; Fiber: 2g

TAJÍN-CITRUS VINAIGRETTE *page 149*

CHAPTER 8

DRESSINGS

Tie your salad together by using one of these 20 foolproof, flavorful salad dressing recipes. Always use fresh citrus fruits, and use high-quality oil as much as possible, for maximum flavor impact. Some of these dressings can last at least 3 days in the refrigerator, and many others can last up to 2 weeks at room temperature, so they're easy to make ahead to have on hand when you need them!

LEMON VINAIGRETTE

MAKES ABOUT 1 CUP

PREP TIME: 5 MINUTES

VEGAN, GLUTEN-FREE, NUT-FREE, DAIRY-FREE

This is *the* foolproof go-to salad dressing. It's simple and to the point—fresh lemon juice, high-quality extra-virgin olive oil, vinegar, and a dash of salt and pepper. When in doubt, go with a lemon vinaigrette.

1 cup high-quality extra-virgin olive oil B
Grated zest of ½ lemon A
Juice of ½ lemon (about 1 to
    1½ tablespoons juice) A
1 to 1½ tablespoons white wine vinegar,
    rice vinegar, or sherry vinegar A
Pinch salt
Pinch freshly ground black pepper

Add the ingredients to a small bowl, Mason jar, or salad dressing shaker. Whisk to combine, or shake the bottle. This dressing will last up to 2 weeks at room temperature. Give it a shake before dressing a salad with it.

PER SERVING (2 TABLESPOONS)

Calories: 217; Fat: 25g; Sodium: 20mg;
Carbohydrates: 0g; Protein: 0g; Fiber: 0g

ASIAN SOY VINAIGRETTE

MAKES ABOUT 1¼ CUPS

PREP TIME: 5 MINUTES

VEGETARIAN, NUT-FREE, DAIRY-FREE

The smell of this soy vinaigrette is amazing. This is one of the most aromatic dressings in the book, and that's because it's loaded with fresh citrus and fresh ginger. The flavor combination is vibrant and light, and it's a fantastic addition to the Asian-inspired salads in chapter 3.

1 cup low-sodium soy sauce **B**
3 tablespoons sesame oil **B**
1 tablespoon honey **E**
1 (1-inch) piece fresh ginger, grated **A**
¼ teaspoon grated orange zest **A**
¼ teaspoon grated lime zest **A**
½ tablespoon minced chives
    or scallions **A**
Small handful fresh cilantro leaves **A**
Pinch salt
Pinch freshly ground black pepper
Togarashi seasoning (optional,
    for additional heat and spice)

Add the ingredients to a small bowl, Mason jar, or salad dressing shaker. Whisk to combine, or shake the bottle. This dressing will last up to 2 weeks at room temperature. Give it a shake before dressing a salad with it.

INGREDIENT TIP: Togarashi seasoning is a Japanese spice blend typically made up of seven spices, including ground red chile, ground sansho pepper, sesame seeds, roasted orange peel, and ground ginger. Add a dash of it to give dressing that extra-special something-something.

PER SERVING (2 TABLESPOONS)
Calories: 58; Fat: 5g; Sodium: 1,461mg;
Carbohydrates: 4g; Protein: 2g; Fiber: 0g

HERB VINAIGRETTE

MAKES ABOUT 1½ CUPS

PREP TIME: 5 MINUTES

VEGAN, GLUTEN-FREE, NUT-FREE, DAIRY-FREE

This dressing is loaded with fresh herbs for maximum aromatics. It's simple and earthy, divine with fall ingredients such as pumpkin or butternut squash. It's also a great way to add freshness and lighten up any salad.

1 cup high-quality extra-virgin olive oil B

2 or 3 tablespoons white wine vinegar, rice vinegar, or sherry vinegar A

¼ cup loosely packed fresh parsley leaves, minced A

¼ cup loosely packed fresh cilantro leaves, minced A

¼ cup loosely packed fresh oregano leaves, minced A

Pinch salt

Pinch freshly ground black pepper

Add the ingredients to a small bowl, Mason jar, or salad dressing shaker. Whisk to combine, or shake the bottle. This dressing will last up to 2 weeks at room temperature. Give it a shake before dressing a salad with it.

PER SERVING (2 TABLESPOONS)

Calories: 150; Fat: 17g; Sodium: 13mg; Carbohydrates: 1g; Protein: 0g; Fiber: 1g

TAJÍN-CITRUS VINAIGRETTE

MAKES ABOUT 1¼ CUPS

PREP TIME: 5 MINUTES

VEGAN, GLUTEN-FREE, NUT-FREE, DAIRY-FREE

For a tangy flavor explosion used heavily in Latin-inspired salads, make this Tajín-citrus vinaigrette. Chili powder and fresh lime make a killer combination.

½ cup high-quality extra-virgin olive oil B
½ cup grapeseed oil B
¼ cup loosely packed fresh cilantro leaves A
1 teaspoon Tajín S
Juice of ½ orange A
Juice of ½ lime A
Pinch salt
Pinch freshly ground black pepper

Add the ingredients to a small bowl, Mason jar, or salad dressing shaker. Whisk to combine, or shake the bottle. This dressing will last up to 2 weeks at room temperature. Give it a shake before dressing a salad with it.

SUBSTITUTION TIP: You can use red chili powder in place of the Tajín. If you do, increase the amount of lime juice used.

PER SERVING (2 TABLESPOONS)
Calories: 185; Fat: 21g; Sodium: 16mg; Carbohydrates: 1g; Protein: 0g; Fiber: 0g

HONEY-MUSTARD VINAIGRETTE

MAKE ABOUT 1¼ CUPS

PREP TIME: 5 MINUTES

VEGETARIAN, GLUTEN-FREE, NUT-FREE, DAIRY-FREE

Sweet, tangy, and packed with flavor—this is a fantastic vinaigrette, as well as a great marinade for fish. For maximum results, use whole-grain mustard instead of the processed bottle kind.

1 small garlic clove **A**

1 cup high-quality extra-virgin olive oil **B**

2 or 3 tablespoons white wine vinegar, rice vinegar, or sherry vinegar **A**

½ tablespoon whole-grain mustard **E**

½ tablespoon honey **E**

Pinch salt

Pinch freshly ground black pepper

1. With the heel of your hand or the flat side of a knife, apply a bit of pressure to the garlic to slightly crush it. Slice the crushed clove.

2. Add the garlic to a small bowl, Mason jar, or salad dressing shaker along with the olive oil, vinegar, mustard, honey, salt, and pepper. Whisk to combine, or shake the bottle. This dressing will last up to 2 weeks at room temperature. Give it a shake before dressing a salad with it.

PER SERVING (2 TABLESPOONS)

Calories: 179; Fat: 20g; Sodium: 31mg; Carbohydrates: 1g; Protein: 0g; Fiber: 0g

HONEY-ORANGE VINAIGRETTE

MAKES ABOUT 1½ CUPS

PREP TIME: 5 MINUTES

VEGETARIAN, GLUTEN-FREE, NUT-FREE, DAIRY-FREE

The combination of honey and citrus—often found in Asian and Middle Eastern dishes—creates a balanced, vibrant salad dressing.

1 cup high-quality extra-virgin olive oil B
Grated zest of 1 large orange A
Juice of 1 large orange A
1 tablespoon honey E
1 small garlic clove, minced A
Pinch salt
Pinch freshly ground black pepper

Add the ingredients to a small bowl, Mason jar, or salad dressing shaker. Whisk to combine, or shake the bottle. This dressing will last up to 2 weeks at room temperature. Give it a shake before dressing a salad with it.

PER SERVING (2 TABLESPOONS)
Calories: 153; Fat: 17g; Sodium: 12mg;
Carbohydrates: 2g; Protein: 0g; Fiber: 0g

CILANTRO-LIME DRESSING

MAKES ABOUT 1¼ CUPS
PREP TIME: 5 MINUTES
VEGAN, GLUTEN-FREE, NUT-FREE, DAIRY-FREE

Combining high-quality oils, fresh lime juice, and fresh cilantro leaves is a simple way to load a salad with maximum flavor while using minimal ingredients.

¾ cup grapeseed oil B
¼ cup high-quality extra-virgin olive oil B
Grated zest of 2 limes A
Juice of 2 limes A
¼ cup loosely packed fresh cilantro leaves A
Pinch salt
Pinch freshly ground black pepper

Add the ingredients to a small bowl, Mason jar, or salad dressing shaker. Whisk to combine, or shake the bottle. This dressing will last up to 2 weeks at room temperature. Give it a shake before dressing a salad with it.

PER SERVING (2 TABLESPOONS)
Calories: 190; Fat: 21g; Sodium: 16mg; Carbohydrates: 1g; Protein: 0g; Fiber: 0g

BUTTERMILK-POPPY DRESSING

MAKES ABOUT 1 CUP
PREP TIME: 5 MINUTES
VEGETARIAN, GLUTEN-FREE, NUT-FREE

Tangy buttermilk combined with crunchy poppy seeds makes for a creamy, flavorful dairy-based salad dressing.

⅔ cup buttermilk B
⅓ cup full-fat sour cream E
1 tablespoon honey E
Grated zest of ½ lemon A
Juice of ½ lemon A
1 tablespoon poppy seeds S
Pinch salt
Pinch freshly ground black pepper

Add the ingredients to a small bowl, Mason jar, or salad dressing shaker. Whisk to combine, or shake the bottle. Seal the container and refrigerate for up to 4 days.

PER SERVING (2 TABLESPOONS)

Calories: 44; Fat: 3g; Sodium: 46mg; Carbohydrates: 4g; Protein: 1g; Fiber: 0g

GINGER-MISO VINAIGRETTE

MAKES ABOUT 1¼ CUPS

PREP TIME: 5 MINUTES

VEGETARIAN, NUT-FREE, DAIRY-FREE

This isn't just a salad dressing—it's also what your doctor ordered. Fresh ginger, white miso paste, garlic, and honey are all superfoods, and they're in this dressing. White miso is the mildest type of miso; it is made by quickly fermenting soy beans, rice, or barley. This dressing is super healthy, super yummy, and super perfect with Asian dishes.

1 large garlic clove **A**
¾ cup grapeseed, vegetable, or canola oil **B**
¼ cup sesame oil **B**
2 tablespoons miso paste **E**
1 (1-inch) piece fresh ginger, grated **A**
1 teaspoon honey **E**
Pinch salt
Pinch freshly ground black pepper

1. With the heel of your hand or the flat side of a knife, apply a bit of pressure to the garlic to slightly crush it. Slice the crushed clove.

2. Add the garlic to a small bowl, Mason jar, or salad dressing shaker along with the grapeseed oil, sesame oil, miso paste, ginger, honey, salt, and pepper. Whisk to combine, or shake the bottle. Seal the container and refrigerate for up to 4 days.

PER SERVING (2 TABLESPOONS)
Calories: 203; Fat: 22g; Sodium: 144mg; Carbohydrates: 2g; Protein: 0g; Fiber: 0g

PESTO DRESSING

Pesto is a great addition to Mediterranean dishes and pasta salads. Filled with fresh herbs and lemon, this dressing brightens any dish in a healthy way.

1 tablespoon white wine vinegar, rice vinegar, or sherry vinegar **A**

Juice of ½ lemon **A**

½ cup loosely packed fresh basil leaves **A**

¼ cup loosely packed fresh parsley leaves **A**

1 large garlic clove **S**

Pinch salt

Pinch freshly ground black pepper

1 teaspoon red pepper flakes (optional) **S**

1 cup high-quality extra-virgin olive oil **B**

Place the vinegar, lemon juice, basil, parsley, garlic, salt, pepper, and red pepper flakes (if using) in a blender. Pulse a few times to incorporate the ingredients. With the blender running, slowly pour in the oil. This helps thicken the dressing and bring it together. Transfer to a sealed container, Mason jar, or dressing shaker. The dressing can be refrigerated for up to 3 days, but it is best if eaten within 1 day of preparation.

PER SERVING (2 TABLESPOONS)
Calories: 146; Fat: 17g; Sodium: 13mg; Carbohydrates: 1g; Protein: 0g; Fiber: 0g

CREAMY CHIPOTLE DRESSING

MAKES ABOUT 1¼ CUPS

PREP TIME: 5 MINUTES

VEGETARIAN, NUT-FREE

This is a two-for-one—it's a salad dressing but also a rich dip for chips. Chipotle chiles in adobo sauce are commonly found in the Latin food aisle of big supermarkets, and they're one of the most flavorful ingredients. A little packs a flavor punch. A little extra kicks up the heat level. For a lighter dressing, replace some of the sour cream and mayonnaise with Greek yogurt.

⅔ cup sour cream **B**

⅓ cup mayonnaise **E**

1 or 2 chipotle peppers in adobo sauce (amount will depend on your heat preference) **S**

Grated zest of 1 lime **A**

Juice of 1 lime **A**

Pinch salt

Pinch freshly ground black pepper

Place all the ingredients in a blender. Blend until completely smooth. Taste and adjust the seasonings as needed. Transfer to a resealable container, Mason jar, or dressing shaker and refrigerate for up to 4 days.

PER SERVING (2 TABLESPOONS)

Calories: 67; Fat: 6g; Sodium: 144mg; Carbohydrates: 3g; Protein: 1g; Fiber: 0g

AVOCADO-YOGURT DRESSING

MAKES ABOUT 1 CUP

PREP TIME: 5 MINUTES

VEGETARIAN, GLUTEN-FREE, NUT-FREE

This dressing is loaded with healthy fats and protein, and it adds a smooth, creamy texture to any salad.

1 large, ripe avocado, pitted B
½ cup plain Greek yogurt E
¼ cup loosely packed cilantro leaves A
¼ cup loosely packed parsley leaves A
Grated zest of 1 lime A
Juice of 1 lime A
1 small garlic clove S
Pinch salt
Pinch freshly ground black pepper

Place all the ingredients in a blender. Blend until completely smooth. Taste and adjust the seasonings as needed. Transfer to a resealable container, Mason jar, or dressing shaker. The dressing can be refrigerated for up to 2 days, but it is best if eaten right away.

PER SERVING (2 TABLESPOONS)
Calories: 64; Fat: 5g; Sodium: 29mg; Carbohydrates: 4g; Protein: 2g; Fiber: 2g

LEMON-TAHINI DRESSING

MAKES ABOUT 1 CUP

PREP TIME: 5 MINUTES

VEGAN, DAIRY-FREE

This is a healthy, lemony dressing made with tahini, fresh lemon, high-quality extra-virgin olive oil, garlic, and fresh parsley. Sesame is a common ingredient in both Middle Eastern and Asian cuisines, making it a fantastic addition!

¾ cup tahini E
2 tablespoons high-quality extra-virgin
    olive oil B
Juice of 3 lemons (about ½ cup) A
1 small garlic clove S
½ cup loosely packed fresh
    parsley leaves A
Pinch salt
Pinch freshly ground black pepper

Place all the ingredients in a blender. Blend until completely smooth. Taste and season with additional salt, pepper, and lemon juice if needed. If the dressing is too thick, blend in a few tablespoons of water or more lemon juice. Transfer to a resealable container, Mason jar, or dressing shaker and refrigerate for up to 1 week.

INGREDIENT TIP: Tahini is a paste made from ground sesame seeds. It can be found in most supermarkets and in Middle Eastern groceries.

PER SERVING (2 TABLESPOONS)
Calories: 169; Fat: 16g; Sodium: 50mg; Carbohydrates: 6g; Protein: 4g; Fiber: 2g

DILL, LEMON, AND GARLIC
SOUR CREAM DRESSING

MAKES ABOUT 1¼ CUPS
PREP TIME: 5 MINUTES
VEGETARIAN, GLUTEN-FREE, NUT-FREE

Quick, healthy, and loaded with flavor—this sour cream–based dressing with dill, lemon, and garlic adds a ton of bright flavor and creamy texture to salads. It's also an amazing dip for fresh vegetables or chips.

1 cup full-fat sour cream E
¼ cup loosely packed dill sprigs A
Juice of 1 lemon A
1 small garlic clove, minced B
Pinch salt
Pinch freshly ground black pepper

Add the ingredients to a small bowl, Mason jar, or salad dressing shaker. Whisk to combine, or shake the bottle. Seal the container and refrigerate for up to 5 days. The dressing is at its best about 4 hours after making, once the flavors have melded together.

PER SERVING (2 TABLESPOONS)

Calories: 51; Fat: 5g; Sodium: 28mg; Carbohydrates: 2g; Protein: 1g; Fiber: 0g

CHARRED GRAPEFRUIT VINAIGRETTE

MAKES ABOUT 1½ CUPS

PREP TIME: 15 MINUTES / COOK TIME: 5 MINUTES / TOTAL TIME: 20 MINUTES

VEGETARIAN, GLUTEN-FREE, NUT-FREE, DAIRY-FREE

Smoky charred grapefruit is added to this vinaigrette for a more complex, layered salad dressing. It's perfect for salad greens, meats, or seafood dishes!

1 large grapefruit **A**
1 teaspoon sugar
1 to 1½ cups high-quality extra-virgin olive oil **B**
1 teaspoon honey **E**
Pinch salt
Pinch freshly ground black pepper

1. Halve the grapefruit crosswise and sprinkle the flesh evenly with the sugar. If you have a cooking blow torch, brûlée the grapefruit until the sugar has caramelized on top. Alternatively, preheat the broiler. Prepare the grapefruit the same way but also cut a small sliver from the bottom of each half so they will sit upright and the sugared surface will be level under the broiler. Broil for about 5 minutes, or until the sugar has caramelized. Once the grapefruit is cool enough to handle, juice it.

2. Add the grapefruit juice, olive oil, honey, salt, and pepper to a small bowl, Mason jar, or salad dressing shaker. Whisk to combine, or shake the bottle. The dressing will last up to 2 weeks at room temperature. Give it a shake before dressing salad with it.

PER SERVING (2 TABLESPOONS)
Calories: 224; Fat: 25g; Sodium: 12mg; Carbohydrates: 2g; Protein: 0g; Fiber: 0g

ROASTED POBLANO CREMA

MAKES ABOUT 1½ CUPS

PREP TIME: 20 MINUTES / COOK TIME: 10 MINUTES / TOTAL TIME: 30 MINUTES

VEGETARIAN, GLUTEN-FREE, NUT-FREE

This zesty, tangy, creamy salad dressing with roasted poblano chiles, fresh cilantro, fresh lime, and a mixture of sour cream and mayonnaise is also a perfect dip for tortilla chips and goes great with tacos and burritos.

2 large poblano chiles B
1 cup full-fat sour cream B
½ cup mayonnaise E
½ cup loosely packed cilantro leaves A
Grated zest of 1 or 2 limes A
Juice of 1 or 2 limes A
Pinch salt
Pinch freshly ground black pepper

1. Preheat the broiler.

2. Place the poblanos on a baking sheet and broil for about 10 minutes, rotating them every few minutes to get an even char on all sides.

3. Transfer the poblanos to a large resealable bag and seal tightly. Let them sit for about 5 minutes to cool. Once they're cool enough to handle, the skins should peel off easily. Halve the poblanos lengthwise and remove the seeds.

4. Place the poblanos in a blender along with the sour cream, mayonnaise, cilantro, lime zest, lime juice, salt, and pepper. Blend until smooth. Transfer the dressing to a resealable container, Mason jar, or dressing shaker. The dressing can be refrigerated for up to 4 days, but it is best eaten right away.

PER SERVING (2 TABLESPOONS)
Calories: 83; Fat: 7g; Sodium: 92mg; Carbohydrates: 4g; Protein: 1g; Fiber: 0g

CUMIN-MINT YOGURT DRESSING

MAKES ABOUT 1¼ CUPS

PREP TIME: 5 MINUTES

VEGETARIAN, GLUTEN-FREE, NUT-FREE

Take your typical yogurt and amplify it with a couple of simple ingredients—in this case, cumin, fresh lemon, fresh mint, and garlic. This is a perfect complement for Middle Eastern and South Asian dishes.

1 cup full-fat plain Greek yogurt B
1 teaspoon ground cumin S
Grated zest of ½ small lemon A
Juice of ½ small lemon A
¼ cup loosely packed fresh
    mint leaves A
1 small garlic clove, minced S
Pinch salt
Pinch freshly ground black pepper

Place all the ingredients in a blender. Blend until completely smooth. Taste and adjust the seasonings as needed. If the dressing is too thick, blend in a few tablespoons of water or more lemon juice. Transfer to a resealable container, Mason jar, or dressing shaker and refrigerate for up to 4 days.

PER SERVING (2 TABLESPOONS)

Calories: 33; Fat: 2g; Sodium: 40mg;
Carbohydrates: 2g; Protein: 1g; Fiber: 0g

DATE-BALSAMIC VINAIGRETTE

MAKES ABOUT 1½ CUPS
PREP TIME: 5 MINUTES
VEGETARIAN, GLUTEN-FREE, NUT-FREE, DAIRY-FREE

A nice balance of sweet and sour, dates and balsamic vinegar make for a complex, deep salad dressing. It's a great blend of acidic and sweetness.

1 cup high-quality extra-virgin olive oil B
¼ cup cold water
¼ cup white or red balsamic vinegar A
2 cups dates, pitted and roughly chopped A
Juice of 1 lemon A
½ tablespoon Dijon mustard E
1 teaspoon honey E
Pinch salt
Pinch freshly ground black pepper

Place all the ingredients in a blender. Blend until completely smooth. Taste and adjust the seasonings as needed. If the dressing is too thick, blend in a few tablespoons of water or more lemon juice. Transfer to a resealable container, Mason jar, or dressing shaker and refrigerate for up to 1 week.

PER SERVING (2 TABLESPOONS)
Calories: 232; Fat: 17g; Sodium: 21mg;
Carbohydrates: 23g; Protein: 1g; Fiber: 2g

CHIMICHURRI VINAIGRETTE

MAKES ABOUT 2 CUPS
PREP TIME: 5 MINUTES
VEGAN, NUT-FREE, DAIRY-FREE

Feel like a real Argentinean cowboy with this fresh herb, oil, and lemon vinaigrette. This dressing will add a lot of freshness and bright color to any salad. It's also perfect as a marinade and garnish for steak and seafood.

1½ cups high-quality extra-virgin olive oil **B**

¼ cup red wine vinegar, white wine vinegar, or white balsamic vinegar **A**

½ cup loosely packed fresh parsley leaves **A**

¼ cup loosely packed fresh cilantro leaves **A**

¼ cup loosely packed fresh basil leaves **A**

Grated zest of 2 lemons **A**

Juice of 2 lemons **A**

1 tablespoon panko bread crumbs **E**

1 large garlic clove **S**

½ teaspoon red pepper flakes **S**

Pinch salt

Pinch freshly ground black pepper

Place all the ingredients in a blender. Pulse until the herbs have broken apart and the dressing turns into an oily paste. If it is too thick, blend in a few tablespoons of water or extra olive oil. Transfer to a resealable container, Mason jar, or dressing shaker and refrigerate for up to 4 weeks.

PER SERVING (2 TABLESPOONS)
Calories: 167; Fat: 19g; Sodium: 17mg; Carbohydrates: 1g; Protein: 0g; Fiber: 0g

CHERMOULA DRESSING

MAKES ABOUT 1½ CUPS

PREP TIME: 10 MINUTES

VEGAN, GLUTEN-FREE, NUT-FREE, DAIRY-FREE

A paste made from extra-virgin olive oil, herbs, preserved lemons, and spices, this decadent North African concoction is a flavor explosion, especially on salads with seafood.

1 cup loosely packed mixed fresh cilantro, mint, and/or parsley leaves **A**

Rind of 1 preserved lemon, minced, or grated zest of 1 lemon **A**

4 garlic cloves, minced **S**

1 cup high-quality extra-virgin olive oil **B**

Juice of 1 preserved lemon or lemon **A**

2 tablespoons paprika **S**

1 tablespoon ground cumin **S**

¼ teaspoon cayenne pepper **S**

¼ teaspoon saffron **A**

Pinch salt

Pinch freshly ground black pepper

For ideal results, use a mortar and pestle to crush the herbs, rind or zest, and garlic. Transfer the mixture to the bowl of a food processor and add the olive oil, lemon juice, paprika, cumin, cayenne pepper, saffron, salt, and pepper. Process until well combined. Alternatively, place all the ingredients together in the bowl of the food processor and process. Transfer the dressing to a resealable container, Mason jar, or dressing shaker and refrigerate for up to 1 week.

INGREDIENT TIP: Saffron is the world's most expensive spice, and it is very potent, so use extremely sparingly—a little goes a very long way. To cut down on cost, use saffron powder as a substitute, or exclude it altogether if you can't find it or it's outside of your budget.

PER SERVING (2 TABLESPOONS)

Calories: 152; Fat: 17g; Sodium: 14mg; Carbohydrates: 1g; Protein: 0g; Fiber: 1g

THE DIRTY DOZEN AND THE CLEAN FIFTEEN™

A nonprofit environmental watchdog organization called Environmental Working Group (EWG) looks at data supplied by the U.S. Department of Agriculture (USDA) and the Food and Drug Administration (FDA) about pesticide residues. Each year it compiles a list of the best and worst pesticide loads found in commercial crops. You can use these lists to decide which fruits and vegetables to buy organic to minimize your exposure to pesticides and which produce is considered safe enough to buy conventionally. This does not mean they are pesticide-free, though, so wash these fruits and vegetables thoroughly.

Dirty Dozen

- Apples
- Celery
- Cherries
- Grapes
- Nectarines
- Peaches
- Pears
- Potatoes
- Spinach
- Strawberries
- Sweet bell peppers
- Tomatoes

In addition to the Dirty Dozen, the EWG added one type of produce contaminated with highly toxic organophosphate insecticides:

- Hot peppers

Clean Fifteen

- Asparagus
- Avocados
- Cabbage
- Cantaloupes (domestic)
- Cauliflower
- Eggplants
- Grapefruits
- Honeydew
- Kiwis
- Mangoes
- Onions
- Papayas
- Pineapples
- Sweet corn
- Sweet peas (frozen)

MEASUREMENT CONVERSIONS

VOLUME EQUIVALENTS (Liquid)

US Standard	US Standard (ounces)	Metric (approximate)
2 tablespoons	1 fl. oz.	30 mL
¼ cup	2 fl. oz.	60 mL
½ cup	4 fl. oz.	120 mL
1 cup	8 fl. oz.	240 mL
1½ cups	12 fl. oz	355 mL
2 cups or 1 pint	16 fl. oz.	475 mL
4 cups or 1 quart	32 fl. oz.	1 L
1 gallon	128 fl. oz.	4 L

OVEN TEMPERATURES

Fahrenheit (F)	Celsius (C) (approximate)
250°F	120°C
300°F	150°C
325°F	165°C
350°F	180°C
375°F	190°C
400°F	200°C
425°F	220°C
450°F	230°C

VOLUME EQUIVALENTS (Dry)

US Standard	Metric (approximate)
⅛ teaspoon	0.5 mL
¼ teaspoon	1 mL
½ teaspoon	2 mL
¾ teaspoon	4 mL
1 teaspoon	5 mL
1 tablespoon	15 mL
¼ cup	59 mL
⅓ cup	79 mL
½ cup	118 mL
⅔ cup	156 mL
¾ cup	177 mL
1 cup	235 mL
2 cups or 1 pint	475 mL
3 cups	700 mL
4 cups or 1 quart	1 L

WEIGHT EQUIVALENTS

US Standard	Metric (approximate)
½ ounce	15 g
1 ounce	30 g
2 ounces	60 g
4 ounces	115 g
8 ounces	225 g
12 ounces	340 g
16 ounces or 1 pound	455 g

RECIPE INDEX

INDEX

ACKNOWLEDGMENTS

To my mom, who taught me how to wash dishes, set the table, chop a basic salad, and eventually cook a full meal. Thank you for teaching me what home feels like, and how sharing meals with friends and family plays into that. Thank you for always being a phone call away for when I *urgently* need your advice on whether adding ABC to XYZ is a good idea, and for listening to my crazy brunch menu ideas.

 To my dad, who will eat literally anything you put in front of him (except spicy food or Brussels sprouts). Thank you for exposing me to different cultures, countries, and experiences from birth. I'm a global citizen because of you. Thank you for keeping me grounded and realistic.

 To my brother, who lit a fire under my a** and made me realize I'm actually pretty okay at cooking, photographing food, and writing recipes. Thank you for being my go-to person and one of the best support networks I have. I would never have gotten this far in my cooking career if it wasn't for you.

 To my "guinea pigs," who willingly taste my food and try my recipes. Food is meaningless unless you can share it with someone you enjoy spending time with. Thank you for putting up with me photographing my culinary concoctions from every angle and (sometimes) letting your food go cold because I was trying to capture *the* perfect shot.

 To Callisto Media, who gave me the opportunity to author this book. Thank you for believing in me, supporting me, and showing me the ropes of being a first-time published cookbook author.

ABOUT THE AUTHOR

Nicole Pavlovsky is a San Francisco-based food blogger, recipe developer, and food photographer. By day, she works in finance at a start-up.

She's nicknamed "Fresh Chef Nikki" for her commitment to making traditional dishes fresh, adding her own modern and global spin on them. Her recipes and photos have landed her a spot on Food Network's Chopped at Home Challenge, features from various high-profile media, and lots of hungry friends and family members in her kitchen. You can find her on Instagram @FreshChefNikki or visit her blog at www.FreshChefNikki.com.

CPSIA information can be obtained
at www.ICGtesting.com
Printed in the USA
BVHW02s1307290318
511488BV00002BC/2/P

9 781641 520317